CONCILIUM

CONCILIUM
ADVISORY COMMITTEE

GREGORY BAUM	*Montreal, QC* Canada
JOSÉ OSCAR BEOZZO	*São Paulo, SP* Brazil
WIM BEUKEN	*Louvain* Belgium
LEONARDO BOFF	*Petrópolis, RJ* Brazil
JOHN COLEMAN	*Los Angeles, CA* USA
CHRISTIAN DUQUOC	*Lyon* France
VIRGIL ELIZONDO	*San Antonio, TX* USA
SEAN FREYNE	*Dublin* Ireland
CLAUDE GEFFRÉ	*Paris* France
NORBERT GREINACHER	*Tübingen* Germany
GUSTAVO GUTIÉRREZ	*Lima* Peru
HERMANN HÄRING	*Tübingen* Germany
WERNER G. JEANROND	*Glasgow* Scotland
JEAN-PIERRE JOSSUA	*Paris* France
MAUREEN JUNKER-KENNY	*Dublin* Ireland
FRANÇOIS KABASELE LUMBALA	*Kinshasa* Dem. Rep. of Congo
NICHOLAS LASH	*Cambridge* England
MARY-JOHN MANANZAN	*Manila* Philippines
ALBERTO MELLONI	*Reggio Emilia* Italy
NORBERT METTE	*Münster* Germany
DIETMAR MIETH	*Tübingen* Germany
JÜRGEN MOLTMANN	*Tübingen* Germany
TERESA OKURE	*Port Harcourt* Nigeria
ALOYSIUS PIERIS	*Kelaniya, Colombo* Sri Lanka
DAVID POWER	*Washington, D.C.* USA
GIUSEPPE RUGGIERI	*Catania* Italy
PAUL SCHOTSMANS	*Louvain* Belgium
JANET MARTIN SOSKICE	*Cambridge* England
ELSA TAMEZ	*San José* Costa Rica
CHRISTOPH THEOBALD	*Paris* France
DAVID TRACY	*Chicago, IL* USA
MARCIANO VIDAL	*Madrid* Spain
ELLEN VAN WOLDE	*Tilburg* Holland

THEOLOGY AND MAGISTERIUM

Edited by

Susan A. Ross and Felix Wilfred

SCM Press · London

Published in 2012 by SCM Press, 3rd Floor, Invicta House, 108–114 Golden Lane,
London EC1Y 0TG.

SCM Press is an imprint of Hymns Ancient & Modern Ltd (a registered charity)
13A Hellesdon Park Road, Norwich NR6 5DR, UK

Copyright © International Association of Conciliar Theology, Madras (India)

www.concilium.in

English translations copyright © 2012 Hymns Ancient & Modern Ltd.

All rights reserved. No part of this publication may be reproduced, stored
in a retrieval system, or transmitted, in any form or by any means,
electronic, mechanical, photocopying or otherwise, without the prior
written permission of the Board of Directors of Concilium.

ISBN 9780334031185

Printed in the UK by
CPI Antony Rowe, Chippenham, Wiltshire

Concilium is published in March, June, August, October, December

Contents

Editorial	7
Bishops and Theologians: Tensions Old and New	15

Part One: Contexts

Magisterium and Theology in Africa ELOI MESSI METOGO	17
The Magisterium and Asian Theologians GEORG EVERS	28
Church, Theology and Magisterium in Latin America AGENOR BRIGHENTI	39
Magisterium and Theology: Principles and Facts ANDRES TORRES QUEIRUGA	51
Theologians and Bishops: Good Procedures Promote Collaboration JAMES A. CORIDEN	64
Teaching as Learning: An Asian View PETER C. PHAN	75

Part Two: Theological Forum

Introduction: Silence in the Church	89
Relations between Truth, Authority, Power and Sacredness in the Church LUIZ CARLOS SUSIN	91

Terrifying Internal Problems. What Theology has to Say
   about Lies 97
SOLANGE LEFEBVRE

Silence and Concealment in the Church in Croatia 102
FRANO PRCELA OP

'Many sources are still inaccessible' 112
HUBERT WOLF, NORBERT RECK

A Tribute to Paul Burns 122

Contributors 125

Editorial

Bishops and Theologians: Tensions Old and New

Theologians and bishops share in the teaching office of the Church in different ways. While bishops serve as shepherds of their flocks and as 'authentic teachers, endowed with the authority of Christ, who preach the faith to the people entrusted to them',[1] the theologian's task has traditionally been described as 'faith seeking understanding', a process described in these words by both Augustine and Anselm. In the words of Professor Elizabeth Johnson, CSJ, 'Theological research does not simply reiterate received doctrinal formulas but probes and interprets them in order to deepen understanding. To do this well, theology throughout history has articulated faith in different thought forms, images, and linguistic expressions. Its work employs all manner of methods and ideas taken from other disciplines in order to shed light on the meaning of faith.'[2]

In recent years, and particularly in 2011, the relationship between bishops and theologians has grown increasingly strained. A recent case in the United States has attracted a great deal of media attention. In 2007, Elizabeth Johnson, a Distinguished Professor of Theology at Fordham University in New York, published *Quest for the Living God: Mapping Frontiers in the Theology of God*. The book was written for a general audience and was widely used in universities and in parish adult education classes. It came to the attention of some US bishops, who communicated their concerns to the US Conference of Catholic Bishops' Committee on Doctrine. Four years later, in March 2011, the Committee issued a statement that asserted that Professor Johnson's book was filled with 'ambiguities, errors, and misrepresentations'.[3] Following the Committee's statement, the Catholic Theological Society of America and the College Theology Society, the two major organizations for professional Catholic theologians in the USA, both issued statements that criticised the Committee's failure to use the process outlined in *Doctrinal Responsibilities,* a set of guidelines that had been developed by the CTSA,

Editorial

the Canon Law Society of America (CLSA) and the US Bishops themselves in 1989, and for their serious misreading of Johnson's text.[4] After a lengthy response by Johnson in June 2011, the Committee on Doctrine reiterated its criticisms in October 2011, along with some new ones. Johnson, the Committee said, did not 'begin with faith', and her theology seriously misrepresented the Catholic tradition's understanding of God as Father and as impassible.[5] Johnson issued a brief statement saying that she still disagreed with the bishops' response.[6]

This process was decidedly not the first to involve the US Committee in critique of a theologian. In autumn 2010, the same Committee issued a statement sharply criticizing the work of two American theologians, Todd A. Salzman and Michael Lawler, for their book *The Sexual Person: Toward a Renewed Catholic Anthropology*, Washington, DC, 2008.[7] We should also note the 2005 statement of the Congregation for the Doctrine of the Faith (hereinafter referred to as CDF). In that year, the CDF announced that it found serious problems in the work of US theologian Roger Haight, SJ, particularly in his book *Jesus Symbol of God*.[8] Four years later, Haight was forbidden by the CDF to teach and write theology; the CDF claimed that his writings caused 'great harm to the faithful.'[9]

This tension is not unique to the USA. In February 2011, a group of German theologians issued a statement entitled *Church 2011: the Need for a New Beginning*.[10] These theologians, now numbering over 270, argue that the Church is in dire need of 'deep-reaching reform' and call for the institutional Church to develop 'the courage of self-reflection.'[11] The statement, unlike those in the USA, does not specifically focus on one particular theological issue or person. Instead, the writers of the letter call for a larger vision of reform in the Church, citing the need for greater 'structures of participation', freedom of conscience, and more attention to the need for a renewed ministry.

One American observer of the situation noted that Auxiliary Bishop Hans-Jochen Jaschke of Hamburg 'spoke out sharply against any attempt to apply pressure on the Catholic Church from outside its structures'. In her blog post, Lisa Fullam, a professor of Theology at the Jesuit School of Theology and Ministry at Santa Clara University, asks whether Catholic theologians are really 'outside' the structure of the Church.[12] On the other side of the ideological spectrum, the US journal *First Things*, which generally reflects a conservative viewpoint, claims that the German theologians want 'Catholicism...to transform itself into another liberal

Editorial

Protestant sect'.[13] Responding to this statement, Father Hans Langendörfer, SJ, the Secretary of the German Bishops' Conference, wrote: 'In a number of issues, the memorandum is in tension with theological beliefs and Church determinations of a highly binding nature.' He continued: 'The relevant issues require urgent further clarification.'[14]

Another example of a theologian facing episcopal criticism is in Spain, where a best-selling life of Jesus was banned in the fall of 2010 because of its threat to traditional Catholic piety. Written by José Antonio Pagola, *Jesus: An Historical Approximation*, a book that argues for God's compassion over God's power, was initially praised by the Pontifical Council for Culture. But apparently after pressure was placed on the CDF by the Spanish Bishops' Conference, copies of the book were withdrawn from sale, although digital copies are available online. Pagola coms from the Basque region, an area which is described as a 'hotbed of dangerous libertinism'. Thirty Spanish theologians have gone on record in support of Pagola.[15]

Around the globe, there have been many other incidents of tension and conflict between bishops and theologians. Readers may recall the case of Ivone Gebara, a Brazilian religious sister who was silenced and forced to go to Europe for 're-education' for two years in 1995. Gebara returned to Brazil after her 'exile' and has continued to publish.[16] Jon Sobrino, SJ, a Spanish priest who has lived in El Salvador for decades, and an author of many works in liberation theology, was told by the CDF in 2007 that his work was 'erroneous or dangerous and may cause harm to the faithful'.[17]

Over the last 30 years, theologians have been excommunicated (Tissa Balasuriya), removed from their positions (Hans Küng, Charles Curran, Roger Haight), been ordered to silence and/or re-education (Ivonne Gebara), subjected to Vatican investigation (Edward Schillebeeckx) and, as noted above, had their work subjected to official reprimand. These actions have usually been taken to 'protect the faithful' from what some bishops see as dangerous ideas that can lead the faithful astray.

This issue of *Concilium* seeks to explore and probe more deeply into this troubled relationship, as in previous issues. Only 50 years ago, Catholic theology was a largely closed discipline taught by priest–professors in seminaries controlled either by religious orders of men or by dioceses. Theologians were trained in pontifical universities and were part of the same clerical communities as their bishops. But Vatican II opened up the ranks of theology to the laity. Universities began teaching theology as an

Editorial

academic discipline, theologians no longer sought *imprimaturs* for their work, and an increasingly well-educated laity sought to explore theological ideas once far beyond their reach.[18] These developments have not been universally well-received by the Vatican or by various bishops. Responses from the non-theologian laity are divided. A quick reading of on-line blogs in response to the 'Johnson affair' shows some extremists defending the bishops against the 'witch-coven' that Johnson is said to lead; the more moderate comments suggest that it is the role of the faithful simply to obey their bishops. On the other hand, a number of writers discuss how transforming Johnson's work has been for them, and many also point out how important it is that theologians should explore new territory.

Certainly tensions between bishops and theologians are nothing new; they date back to the earliest years of the Church. We need only recall the problems that Gnosticism and Arianism posed to the Church's teaching. These theological positions ironically served a valuable purpose in forcing the bishops of the Church to make clear what Christian belief really was. But we must also remember that some theologians, such as Origen, who was originally condemned for his views, have found some measure of affirmation in later years. Some of St Thomas Aquinas's propositions were condemned shortly after his death in 1274, and St Teresa of Avila was called before the Inquisition. Yet today both are revered with the highest title given to a theologian: Doctor of the Church. Just over 100 years ago, the condemnation of Modernism resulted in many theologians losing their academic positions. Some of the views expressed by these theologians would later be officially accepted by the Roman magisterium at Vatican II. Henri de Lubac, SJ, Yves Congar, OP, and John Courtney Murray, SJ were silenced in the years before Vatican II, although Murray later went on to become the chief architect of the council's *Declaration on Religious Liberty*.

Vatican documents over the last 25 years have discussed the significance of the relationship between bishops and theologians. In *Donum Veritatis* (1990), we read that: '…even when collaboration takes place under the best conditions, the possibility cannot be excluded that tensions may arise between the theologian and the magisterium. The meaning attributed to such tensions and the spirit with which they are faced are not matters of indifference. If tensions do not spring from hostile and contrary feelings, they can become a dynamic factor, a stimulus to both the magisterium and theologians to fulfill their respective roles while practising dialogue. In the

Editorial

dialogue, a two-fold rule should prevail. When there is a question of the communion of faith, the principle of the "unity of truth" (*unitas veritatis*) applies. When it is a question of differences which do not jeopardize this communion, the "unity of charity" (*unitas caritatis*) should be safeguarded.' (25–6)

The editors of this issue and the contributors wholeheartedly support this call for charity on the part of bishops and theologians in their dealings with each other.

This volume of *Concilium* takes an international approach to this issue. While much of the 'heat and light' surrounding the bishop–theologian relationship may be more evident in the global North, the global South is not without its own share of tensions. Eloi Messi Metogo of Cameroon writes about the feelings of frustration on the part of many African theologians who find that their efforts to inculturate the Christian message fully in the African context are not taken seriously by Rome. It is only in the last fifty years that significant numbers of bishops are themselves African. Metogo observes that one of the major statements issued by Rome following the 1994 African Synod had exactly *one* reference to an African theologian; the rest were all to Western or papal documents. There is, he notes, a mixture of confidence and mistrust among African theologians as African efforts to inculturate the Gospel fully seem to face a Eurocentric bias.

Georg Evers, for many years the Director of the Asia Desk of the Missiological Institute of Missio in Aachen, Germany, writes about some of the central concerns of Asian theologies: a holistic world-view and an affinity with negative theology, in a religiously pluralistic context. Asian theologies tend to rely more on narratives and myths than on philosophical speculation, which is far more the case in the global North. Evers argues that the kind of 'bilingual' approach taken by Asian theologies is enriching to the tradition. Theologians such as Anthony de Mello, Tissa Balasuriya, and Jemin Ri, as well as the European theologian Jacques Dupuis, SJ, have come under suspicion, if not condemnation by Rome. Like Metogo, Evers would like to see a truly local theology that is in serious dialogue with the religious traditions of Asia and a greater encouragement to theologians engaged in such conversations.

Angenor Brighenti, from Brazil, acknowledges that the relationship between theologians and the magisterium in Latin America has been conflictive and tense for some time. Although some have declared that liberation theology is no longer the force that it was years ago, Brighenti argues for its continued vitality, despite the many rebukes it has received from Rome, which have prohibited it from maturing. Liberation theology is always practised from a position in the Church, not outside it. He notes that theology can be seen from one perspective as based in an essential difference between the clergy and the faithful, but he argues for another, grounded in Vatican II, that sees the theological task as a common search for truth.

From Spain, Andres Torres Queiruga describes a situation where a strongly authoritarian episcopacy has focused on censuring theologians and texts. Torres Queiruga argues that there is a potential for a renewed relationship between bishops and theologians that emphasizes their capacity to enrich each other mutually, which he describes as *perichoresis*. Pope Benedict XVI, he notes, has emphasized the importance of reason and its application to the faith. Torres Queiruga describes the two greatest challenges to the relationship between bishops and theologians as the temptation to power when theologians are 'demonized', and the need to re-develop a sense of the sacramental character of the *whole* Church, not only the hierarchy.

From the United States, James Coriden, a member of both the Catholic Theological Society of America (CTSA) and the Canon Law Society of America (CLSA), affirms the need for unity among the faithful, and points out that bishops and theologians share an ecclesial unity. Coriden summarizes the process that resulted in *Doctrinal Responsibilities* in 1989.[19] This significant document, developed over the course of seven years by the CTSA, the CLSA, and approved by the US Catholic Bishops, describes a process that bishops and theologians can use when there is conflict or disagreement. This process was not used in the 'Johnson affair', to the dismay of many theologians. The Committee on Doctrine of the US Conference of Catholic Bishops (USCCB) argued that it was designed for issues within individual dioceses, not for conflicts that are more national in scope. Coriden then comments on a new protocol suggested by the USCCB Committee on Doctrine. While noting that it is helpful to have a protocol where the process is public, Coriden observes that the new process is only made known to the theologian potentially under investigation at the third step, and that, by contrast, *Doctrinal Responsibilities* is dialogical from the outset. Coriden calls for continued conversation among the groups involved to guarantee a process that respects the unique teaching gifts of

Editorial

bishops and theologians.

Peter Phan, a native of Vietnam and currently teaching at Georgetown University, draws on his own Asian roots to suggest a different approach to the issue, seeing bishops and theologians as 'learners' in common. Phan reminds his readers of Jesus' own role as a learner, in his own education, from others in his ministry, and from the Father. He then turns to Confucian traditions to show that Confucius saw life as a continual and unending process of learning. He notes that Jesus and Confucius teach on the basis of what they have learned and their own personal experiences of learning. He suggests that bishops and theologians should consider engaging in learning together as a way of understanding their faith and each other.

The Theological Forum for this issue, edited by Regina Ammicht Quinn, reflects on 'Silence in the Church'. Theologians approach this topic from three different geographic and cultural perspectives: Brazil, Canada and Croatia. Their common concern is the question: Why do we sometimes hear a special kind of silence, an ear-splitting silence, when different kinds of abuse should be addressed? This might be sexual abuse, but it also can be abuse of power, abuse of the church's mission to proclaim not its own reputation but the liberating Gospel. How do these silences relate to power and authority (Luiz Carlos Susin)? What is the significance of the issue of truth and lies (Solange Lefebvre)? And how does this problem appear in a difficult political context (Frano Prcela)? This reflection is complemented by an interview with the Church historian Hubert Wolf on Pius XII and the beatification process.

As this issue was being completed, we learned of the death of our esteemed colleague Paul Burns, who worked with *Concilium* for many years as translator from Spanish and French to English. We offer a brief tribute to his work and collegiality. His contributions and especially his company will be greatly missed by the *Concilium* community.

The editors offer their deepest thanks to the following for their helpful suggestions, assistance with other languages, references, and support: Brent Little and Bill Wilson, both graduate students at Loyola University Chicago; Luiz Carlos Susin, Hille Haker, Maria Clara Bingemer, Diego Irrarazaval, members of the Editorial Board of *Concilium*; Norbert Reck, whose interview with Christian Wolf has added depth to the *Forum*; and the staff of the *Concilium* Secretariat.

Susan A. Ross, Felix Wilfred

Editorial

Notes

1. *Catechism of the Catholic Church* #2034.
2. http://ncronline.org/news/faith-parish/johnson-letter-us-bishops-doctrine-committee.
3. http://www.usccb.org/about/doctrine/publications/upload/statement-quest-for-the-living-god-2011-03-24.pdf.
4. http://www.ctsa-online.org/BOD_statement_committee-on-doctrine.html.
5. http://www.usccb.org/news/2011/11-205e.cfm.
6. http://cnsblog.wordpress.com/2011/10/28/response-from-sister-elizabeth-johnson-to-us-bishops-committee-on-doctrines-latest-statement/.
7. http://old.usccb.org/doctrine/Sexual_Person_2010-09-15.pdf.
8. http://www.vatican.va/roman_curia/congregations/cfaith/documents/rc_con_cfaith_doc_20041213_notification-fr-haight_en.html.
9. http://ncronline.org/node/3046.
10. http://www.memorandum-freiheit.de/?page_id=518.
11. *Ibid..*
12. http://www.commonwealmagazine.org/blog/?p=12120.
13. http://www.firstthings.com/onthesquare/2011/03/the-chutzpa-of-the-german-theologians.
14. http://www.indcatholicnews.com/news.php?viewStory=17625.
15. http://www.scribd.com/doc/53844267/The-Tablet-UK-March-26-2011-Article-about-Jose-Pagola-s-JESUS-Book.
16. http://www.docstoc.com/docs/55769790/Rome-moves-to-silence-Brazils-Gebara%28controversial-feminist-theologian-Sister-Ivone-Gebara%29.
17. http://www.vatican.va/roman_curia/congregations/cfaith/documents/rc_con_cfaith_doc_20061126_notification-sobrino_en.html.
18. For an insightful volume on liberal Catholicism, see Mary Jo Weaver, ed., *What's Left: Liberal American Catholics*, Bloomington, 1999.
19. http://old.usccb.org/doctrine/publications.shtml.

Part One: Contexts

Magisterium and Theology in Africa

ELOI MESSI METOGO

There is general agreement that the collection of essays entitled *Des prêtres noirs s'interrogent*[1] was the starting-point of African theology. However weak and inadequate it may be in certain respects, this theology has made an important contribution to the emergence of a local magisterium which does much more than merely rubber-stamp papal and conciliar teachings. It is noteworthy that two of the symposium's authors, Robert Dosseh and Robert Sastre, have become bishops, in Togo and Benin respectively. The same is true of leading theologians such as Tarcisse Tshibangu (Democratic Republic of the Congo) and Anselme Sanon (Burkina Faso). That does not mean that relations between the bishops and African theologians are without strain. We must also remember the warnings to African theologians from the Roman magisterium addressed to bishops and theologians, or certain opinions on African theology. The historic event of the first African synod, which gave rise to a rich crop of pronouncements on the present topic, serve as a guideline for this article, which will end with some observations on the essential cooperation between the magisterium and theologians in order to ensure the creation and credibility of an African Catholicity properly speaking.

I African magisterium and theology

There was an African magisterium in 1956, when *Des prêtres noirs s'interrogent* was published. For the most part, it was still exercised by bishops of non-African origin. Bishops of local origin were still few and far between, and Bishop Paul Etoga, René Graffin's auxiliary in Yaoundé (Cameroun) from 1955, was probably the first African bishop in French-speaking black Africa. This magisterium was expressed by Archbishop Marcel Lefebvre of Dakar, Apostolic Delegate for French-speaking black Africa, as intermediary, in a letter to the authors prefacing the collective work.[2] The text of this preface deserves a detailed study which would be out of place here. While encouraging consideration of the 'problems of the African apostolate by Africans', the Apostolic Delegate refers to 'the doctrine of the Church' with regard to the introduction of aspects of local cultures (song, dance, painting, sculpture, and traditional ceremonies related to birth, initiation, marriage and death) in the Church's liturgy. Apart from song, painting and sculpture, the other elements involve risks of syncretism, immorality and fetishism or superstition. He praises the Catholic order and discipline which are sadly lacking in 'churches not in union with Peter'. The Church is beautiful because it possesses the 'splendour of order', which is definable as 'unity in diversity', and not as 'uniformity' or 'anarchy'. But this unity is no different from the unity produced by nature which 'carefully ensures that each being is kept in its due specificity and variety while maintaining a profound unity joining species and type, type and kingdom, together'. The final paragraph describes an unfamiliar Trinity in which the Church replaces the Holy Spirit and is given the mission of 'sanctifying all creatures in order to lead them to God through Jesus Christ'. This text obviously jettisons the notion of an African theology that might well endanger the 'unity of faith and everyday life' guaranteed by Peter 'in the context of ecclesiastical discipline'. At Vatican II, African bishops of foreign origin criticised what had become the patriarchate of the West and called for a return to the patriarchal structures of the first millennium. Unfortunately this proposal was not taken up.[3]

John Paul II convoked the first African synod on 6 January 1989. It prompted intense preparatory research and reflection. Three European theologians, Maurice Cheza, Henri Derroitte and René Luneau, had the brilliant idea of spreading knowledge of the teaching of the African bishops from 1969 to 1991 on the five synodal topics: evangelization, inculturation, interreligious dialogue, justice and peace, and means of social communication.[4] The *terminus a quo* corresponded to the date of Paul VI's historical visit to Uganda (October 1969), and of the foundation of the Symposium of the Bishops' Conferences of Africa and Madagascar (SCEAM), which was the leading church body of that kind in Africa. It was not possible to take things further than 1991 when planning a functional instrument long before the synod opened. During this period covering almost the entire interval between the end of the Second Vatican Council (1965) and the celebration of the African synod (1994), there was a striking identity of views between the magisterium and theologians with regard to sensitive questions otherwise suspect in the eyes of the Church's central government: the inculturation of marriage, reconciliation, the Eucharist, the ordination of married men for the spiritual support of communities and to provide for the celebration of the sacraments, the introduction of lay ministers, the revision of relations between Rome and local churches, and the development of African theology.

Difficulties with regard to the subject of Christian marriage in Africa are concerned not with doctrine (unity, indissolubility, sacramentality), but with discipline and pastoral work. Marriage is a cultural reality which is not practised and experienced in the same way among all nations. As it happens, it is the concern of Africans to Christianize this reality in their own circumstances, to say how and when marriage is concluded validly and becomes indissoluble. This responsibility of discernment and decision should be entrusted to local bishops' conferences (cf. pp. 157; 169–78; 202–3). Why not take into account, in respect of the practice of the sacrament of reconciliation and penance, the communal dimension of reconciliation which is so prized in African tradition, instead of putting all the emphasis on individual confession (cf. pp. 161–9)? What are Africans to make of a Eucharist which excludes local food, 'the fruit of the earth and of human labour' (cf. pp. 157–60)? Forced to deal with the urgently problematical prospect of a Church without priests, the bishops asked the Holy See for permission, 'for the survival and vitalization of Christian communities', to ordain 'certain married Christians carefully chosen from among those leading worthy and exemplary lives. This would enable them to answer fundamental pastoral demands', for the people of God 'are entitled' to the spiritual support of their pastors and the sacraments, especially the Eucharist, 'the source and goal of evangelization'. They could not understand why those who build and compose the community cannot preside over the Eucharist or give absolution (cf. pp. 68–72). According to the teaching of Vatican II, the marginalization of the laity runs counter to the Church as communion: 'Every Christian has a profound share in the life and mission of the Church by virtue of the common association of all the faithful in the mystery of Redemption by baptism and the other sacraments'. Laypeople can participate in the exercise of pastoral duties according to the circumstances and needs of local churches, without any harm to the apostolic ministry, which itself belongs to the ecclesial communion in which we are all missionary disciples (cf. pp. 103–6). The theology of the local Church rediscovered at Vatican II calls for the revision of relations with Rome. Local churches are not fragments of the Church, for 'the universal Church subsists in and through these local churches'. If the universal Church is not to be impoverished, we have to acknowledge the legitimacy of cultural and legal pluralism, and the principle of subsidiarity. Africans are not Latin Christians. They are entitled to the same degree of trust as the western churches which have enjoyed a period 'of two thousand years in which to mislead and make mistakes' (cf. pp. 98–9; 137–8; 140–3; 144; 154–5). The bishops have encouraged theological research and inculturation. The untiring labours of exegetes and theologians has enabled great progress to be made in the formulation of doctrine regarding divine Revelation, but this work has to be continuous, since 'theology tries to express and explain Revelation, without ever succeeding totally and perfectly in this task'. The Church has had a plurality of theological schools and systems; the task of African theologians is to consider the Gospel message in their specific social and cultural context, 'instead of blindly following western theologians' (cf. pp. 125–7; 155–6). It has to be acknowledged that theologians 'exercise an authentic ministry' in pastoral and missionary work (p. 68).

These powerful statements and proposals by the bishops certainly emanate from a process of dialogue with theologians at the diocesan level, in Episcopal conferences and in SCEAM, with its Theological Committee. This freedom of expression and assertion was repeated during the 1994 synod in the reports of Cardinal Thiandoum and the bishops' addresses and interventions.[5] But how are we to explain the reservations of Bishop Ngoyagoye in his preface to this impressive collection of viewpoints: 'A serious problem is concealed behind these few questions (and others too not posed here): that of the relationship that should exist between the bishops' word and the thinking of African theologians.' In Africa there is a constantly growing number of teachers and researchers in the major seminaries and higher institutes of research and education. But as yet the impact of their common thinking does not seem to stand out against a past that is still not inculturated. There is no framework of meeting and exchange but what some people are not slow to call a repetitive form of episcopal discourse. 'It is not a question of blaming ourselves for the problem but of becoming aware of privileged occasions that the next synod could provide to ensure the theological and spiritual health and richness of Africa' (p. 12). Does this mean that a number of bishops do not share the abovementioned thinking on 'provocative questions' in relations between the universal Church and local churches?[6] We may reply in the affirmative by recalling that, at the 1994 synod, an 'African bishop incapable of restraint' did not 'scruple to declare that there were no African theologians'.[7] In fact, 'certain bishops had tried to keep certain theologians in the background'.[8] For Jean-Marc Ela, the theologians had just been sidelined even though they were the source of the very idea which gave rise to the synod (*ibid.*, p. 8). In an attempt to justify this odd behaviour on the part of the African episcopate, one archbishop referred in the assembly hall of a Catholic university to the presence of Father Engelbert Mveng and Jean-Marc Ela as the 'arrival of an historian and sociologist', and then added: 'The bishops are also theologians'. It would seem that the synod made some attempt to 'win credibility by praising the contribution of African theologians in its final message' (J.-M. Ela, *ibid.*, p.13).

II Roman magisterium and African theology

Jan-Marc Ela and Engelbert Mveng offered lively criticisms of the remarks of Cardinal Ratzinger, who then headed the Congregation for the Doctrine of the Faith, on inculturation and more especially on African theology.[9] All Ratzinger could discern in Africa was an array of primitive and tribal religions subject to the attacks of western science and technology. Only Christianity could provide them with means of theological reflection and guarantee them access to modernity in the context of globalization. Christianity itself appears as a universal culture offering its cultural riches to other nations. Apart from the restatement of clichés of colonial ethnology regarding African cultures, we have to combat a conception of Christian universality which excludes the contributions of evangelized peoples to the epiphany of Catholicity, contrary to the teaching of Vatican II on the Church. 'The risen Jesus alone is universal', and no historical Christian figure is 'capable of exhausting the potential implications of his mystery' in all its possible forms of expression. By attacking what he terms 'the dangers of inculturation', Cardinal Ratzinger does not see that inculturation as a living and meaningful expression of the Christian message is a necessity for all churches in a changing world. Inculturation implies cultural and theological pluralism and requires us to abandon a Counter-Reformation Christianity based on 'the Roman magisterium, grace and the sacraments, Scripture and tradition'. More emphatically, by setting himself against authentic inculturation, Cardinal Ratzinger 'wholly restores the tragic alliance of revelation and domination'. Confronted by the whole range of forms of exploitation of their peoples, third-world theologians cannot be content to remain mere commentators on the Catechism of the Catholic Church and the central topics of an ecclesiastical social teaching which is too pusillanimous to denounce the fundamental tenets of a rampant neo-liberalism. They do not see the theology of liberation as an outdated phenomenon.'

According to Maurice Cheza, the ambiance of the 1994 synod was a strange mixture of confidence and mistrust.[10] In general, the Roman Curia relates to Africa only in terms of diocesan reports, *ad limina* visits, national Episcopal conferences, and individual contacts. It is probably rather apprehensive about this major assembly and therefore responds with a variety of gestures of goodwill and even seduction. Many African elements were integrated in the opening liturgy. In his homily, Pope John Paul II said: 'We wish this synod to be a wholly African assembly reaching down to its very roots.' He showed that he had listened attentively to what was said during the working sessions. In a minority, and drowned out as it were by the whole episcopate at other synods, the African bishops were relieved to be together. They felt stronger, more at their ease, and could express themselves freely on African pastoral problems. But surely there was a certain degree of suspicion at work in the very choice of Rome as a venue for the meeting? That tended to stress the distance between the bishops and their people, who could neither support them or put questions to them. Furthermore, everything possible was done to 'avoid the contamination of the bishops at the synod'. They stayed in guarded places. The timetable made it difficult to participate in occasions of unofficial discussion and reflection that were suspect in the opinion of one or other synodal bigwig and were accused by a conservative press of constituting an 'alternative synod'. Moreover, almost all the theologians were marginalized. Finally, during the seventh General Congregation, the intervention of Cardinal Tomko, Prefect of the Congregation for Evangelization, came over as a form of advance censorship: 'Recently certain individuals, basing their opinions on African culture, have once again posed the question of the discipline of priestly celibacy. It is evident that evangelical celibacy is a gift which God does not refuse to those who accept it in faith and with prudence, and to those who deepen it and interiorize it by virtue of a thorough training. It is an evangelical value and not the property of any specific culture. We are grateful to God for the many African priests and religious whose exemplary lives make their people so proud of them.' Here I restrict my comments to remarking that the problem of priestly celibacy is not posed only in the context of African culture, and that this statement is an attempt to evade a serious pastoral problem which I have already mentioned: the vast number of communities in the Latin Church which are deprived of the Eucharist.

A reading of the *Lineamenta* of the first African synod published in 1990 provoked questions which are still relevant. Is there an African magisterium? Almost all the doctrinal references were taken from the Roman magisterium. The post-synodal exhortation *Ecclesia in Africa* contains only a single reference to an African magisterium: to the message of the eighth plenary assembly of SCEAM (19 July 1987) at par. 22, note 22. The propositions put forward by the Fathers of the synod, the most sensitive of which were ignored by the apostolic exhortation, were not as forthright as the actual pronouncements in the plenary sessions. The interventions of several curial cardinals along the lines of the opinion advanced by Cardinal Tomko had their desired effect in that they persuaded the bishops to sideline any theologians suspected of holding progressive views. We might well follow a Zairian lay-person in asking to 'what extent the statements of the bishops at the synod were absolutely…free of any desire to be awarded good marks in Rome', and to continue to benefit from the financial aid of the Vatican by adopting an approach that 'seemed to be increasingly intent on re-establishing a former type of Christianity based on an authoritarian model no longer accepted by many Christians'.[12]

III   The role of the 'theologians' magisterium'

Maurice Cheza remarks that the relationship between African bishops and theologians is 'sometimes characterized by fear and rivalry'.[13] If their very office makes bishops 'doctors of the faith', do they also become professional theologians? Even if they have received a sound theological training, can they afford to do without the cooperation of full-time theologians? Should a theologian restrict himself to repeating the pronouncements of the magisterium?

Melchior Cano's systematization (1509–60) of the 'theological locations' or areas to which theology can look for its arguments 'either to prove or to refute' is a remarkable contribution to the modern conception of theological methodology. It is a corrective to the lack of rigour in scholastic theology, but especially, in taking into consideration not only natural reason but the authority of philosophers and legal experts, and history as a series of supplementary theological *loci*, it 'sanctions the entry of the secular disciplines later known as the humanities into theological argument'.[14] The locations proper to theology include not only the basic instances containing revelation as a whole (Scripture, oral tradition), but certain declarative *loci* which refer to the authority of the Church in general, and to that (especially of general) councils of the Roman Church, that is, of the papal magisterium. Thereafter the authority of older saints, scholastic theologians and canonists is classified as that of probable declarative sources. With Cano, the emphasis shifts from reason to the authority of tradition, which paradoxically favours the doctrinal authority of the Church. 'Accordingly, Cano's works are symptomatic of the enforcement of magisterial reference as a concept in theological activity itself', even though the term 'magisterium' appears only at the end of the eighteenth century and was not used in any of the Church's official texts until Pope Gregory XVI in 1835. By making possible the transition from the scholastic *quaestio* to the adumbration of the *thesis*, and by turning the Church into a theological *locus*, Cano supplied the theoretical bases for a 'progressive dogmatization of the context of faith' (C. Theobald). His approach embodied a certain tension and even conflict which was to emerge in the nineteenth century between Church and university, theology and the sciences or scholarship.[15] This crisis is not insuperable if we allow that the 'ministry of bishops and the ministry of theologians represent different and complementary charisms, under the one Spirit for the well-being of the Church'.[16]

A widespread notion of theology, even in the Church, would have it be a definitively constituted form of knowledge which only has to be handed on. But theology is a reading of the word of God and of the tradition of the Fathers of the Church on the basis of the questions and concerns of the men and women of our own times. Each generation should devote itself to this exercise on its own account. The theologian's role does not consist in repeating what the pope and bishops say. A theologian is a searching individual. Admittedly, 'theology has to see to its relations with the Church', for it is a service rendered to the community of believers; but it 'is a science with all the possibilities of the various forms of human knowledge. It is free to apply its methods and analyses'.[17] Theologians will help the faithful to understand the content of faith and the interpretation of it advanced by the magisterium; they will also suggest new interpretations for those seeking to understand their faith, on the basis of the questions and concerns of the men and women of their own time, both Christians and non-Christians. The role of the magisterium and that of theology are different, but they come together in the service which they render to the same community of faith by virtue of the relevance of their testimony (cf. John Paul II, *ibid.*).

Almost nothing was said at the 1994 synod about the problems posed within the Church in Africa.[18] Many Africans are critical of their bishops, priests and religious. They constitute what is sometimes termed the Church from above instead of the Church from below consisting of the other members of the people of God. Especially when they have academic titles, priests think that they form part of the superior world because of their dual priestly and university initiation. The clergy and religious are accused of insensitivity to people's suffering. The bishops' pronouncements do not correspond to people's actual lives, and more commitment and less talk is expected of them. Intellectuals are also observably losing interest in the institution, all the more so when the clergy think they know everything and speak 'on people's behalf when they really know nothing about them.' They 'are inclined to locate themselves above the living conditions of the mass of people, although they don't even know how much a loaf of bread costs!' This faulty communication between clergy and people tends to subject the latter to the greed and cynicism of 'religious entrepreneurs'. Sad to say, the marginalization of laypeople and women reflects the disdain for people and the macho attitude of the global society. Without minimizing the responsibility of other Christians, we expect theologians to draw our attention to problems that compromise evangelical witness to a serious extent. It is difficult for synodal resolutions (we are waiting for those of the 2009 synod) concerning inculturation, interreligious dialogue, and justice and peace to take shape without the work of theologians who, cooperating with specialists in the social sciences, analyze social phenomena, and put forward models of the Church and pastoral priorities.

The apostolic exhortation *Ecclesia in Africa* (1995) laid considerable stress on instruction in all areas of 'evangelization'. For Pope John Paul II, it conditioned inculturation and witness. Mistrust of scholarly and scientific theology and criticism leads to neglect of theological training in seminaries and Catholic universities. It may be entrusted to unqualified individuals in spite of academic procedures, because they are 'doctrinally sound', or for tribalist or vote-catching reasons. But theology depends and will always depend on dialogue with secular disciplines: philosophy, literature, history, anthropology, sociology, law, economics, cosmology, biology and so on. Authoritarian attitudes, even to the extent of their ignorance of theological tradition and social phenomena, represent a real danger for the future of faith. Have we forgotten that *Ecclesia in Africa* asked bishops to 'improve their knowledge of theological culture' (n° 98)?

Unfortunately the 1994 synod was not a 'context of meeting and exchange', 'a privileged occasion…for the theological fertility of Africa', as Bishop Ngoyagoye so devoutly wished. I shall close this article by citing the wishes of the theologians sidelined from the synodal proceedings that 'the bishops and theologians should arrange carefully prepared meetings to exchange ideas, share common concerns, and work towards common solutions to the many problems facing the Church. Such encounters should occur at all levels: diocesan, national, regional and continental'; that 'the continuation and application of the synod should be the common and universal work of the ecclesiastic community, which includes the ministry of theologians; that 'this work and this common development (*synodos*) of the entire African ecclesial community under the bishops' pastoral responsibility, aided by the competence of African theologians, should lead to a new continental meeting of the Church of Africa: an African Council which will be a much more evident expression of our African identity within the universal unity of the Church' (*Le Synode africain*, p. 391).

Translated by J. G. Cumming

Notes

1. I. e. 'Black Priests Ask Questions'. Paris, 1956, ²2006.
2. *Des prêtres noirs s'interrogent, op. cit.*, pp. 11–4.
3. Cf I. Ndongala Maduku, *Pour des Églises régionales en Afrique*, Paris, 1999, pp. 89–105.
4. *Les évêques d'Afrique parlent (1969–1992), Documents pour le Synode africain,* Paris 1992.
5. See Maurice Cheza (ed.), *Le Synode africain, Histoire et textes,* Paris, 1996, especially pp. 39, 76–7, 100, 124–8, 129–30, 158–9, 199, 203–4, 255, 262.
6. In fact, I have drawn attention to the convergence between the views of the African magisterium and the work of African theologians with regard to these questions, without a detailed account of the sources of the topics: individual bishops, regional or national conferences, and SCEAM. Obviously not all the members of an episcopal conference necessarily share in its official declarations, just as all the Africans teaching

theology do not share the abovementioned magisterial positions. I shall return later to the need for cooperation between bishops and theologians.
7. Jean-Marc Ela, in *Le Synode africain, op.cit.*, 'Préface', p. 13.
8. Propos des théologiens africains', in *Le Synode africain*, p. 391.
9. See J.Ratzinger, *Entretien sur la foi,* Paris, 1985, pp. 241–3. For subsequent developments, see J.-M. Ela, *Repenser la théologie africaine, Le Dieu qui libère*, Paris, 2003, pp. 91–7. Other texts by Cardinal Ratzinger are referred to in note 7 on p. 96.
10. See *Le Synode africain*, pp. 372–4.
11. See *Le Synode africain*, p. 23.
12. 'Réflexions d'une laïque zaïroise', in *Le Synode africain*, pp. 398–9. Madame Sabine Kabunga Madilu offers her opinion of the 64 proposals sent to the Pope by the Fathers of the African synod in May 1994. Zaïre has become the Democratic Republic of the Congo.
13. *Le Synode africain*, p. 382.
14. Thierry Bedouelle, *La théologie*, Paris, 2007, pp. 88–9.
15. See T. Bedouelle, *op.cit.* pp. 89–90.
16. 'Propos des théologiens africains', in *Le Synode africain*, pp. 390–1.
17. Jean-Paul II, 'Rencontre avec un groupe de théologiens allemands le 18.11.1980', *La Documentation catholique*, No. 1798, 21 December 1980, pp. 1161–2.
18. For the following remarks, see M. Cheza, 'Le Synode... et après?'; 'Propos des théologiens africains'; 'Réflexions d'une laïque zaïroise', in *Le Synode africain*, pp. 78–83; 3–391; 393–404.

The Magisterium and Asian Theologians

GEORG EVERS

Before beginning a critical investigation of the relationship between the Roman magisterium and Asian theologians, it is important to state unequivocally that Christians in the Asian minority churches set a very high value on their connection with the Pope and Roman institutions. It is immensely important for Asian Christians, who do not find it easy to define and assert their own identity within the multitude of religions in Asia, to form part of a worldwide ecclesiastical community. The spiritual and financial support experienced through this relationship helps them to construct and run church, educational and charitable facilities, and to train priests, religious and other ecclesiastical professionals. Christians in many Asian countries are subject to persecution and their freedom to practise their religion is often constrained by governments or radical religious groups. In these difficult situations they are thankful for the support which they receive from local nuncios or from Roman instances. Nevertheless, membership of a leading universal Church also means that most local Asian churches (the Philippines are an exception) have not yet achieved the status of autonomous local churches in canon law, but are still dependent in many respects on the Congregation for the Evangelization of Peoples. One way in which this dependence is expressed is the control by the Congregation for Evangelization of Peoples of ecclesiastical training, and accordingly of the work of Asian theologians, which is also more directly controlled by the Congregation for the Doctrine of the Faith.

I The character of Asian theology

Before saying more about the objections of the magisterial to individual aspects of Asian theology, I shall give a summary account of the main concerns and insights developed by Asian theologians in recent decades.[1] A typical feature of the approach favoured by Asian theologians is a fundamentally holistic world-view, and a conviction that all elements are inwardly united, which leads them to work for the preservation or restoration of an original harmony. Unlike Western theology, which often holds to an immanent dualism between body and spirit (mind), subject and object, and nature and grace, Asian theologians proceed from the principle of a fundamental identity, which implies that the most profound transcendent reality is simultaneously the most deeply immanent reality. This results in an attitude of great veneration for the mystery of divine reality and of the cosmos, and an awareness of the restricted capabilities of human language and of human conceptual faculties to express the ultimate reality of the complex of God–world–humanity. Consequently, Asian theologians have a certain affinity with a negative theology which they see as possessing the potential to correct a Western theology that is much more dogmatically self-assured and enamoured of conceptualization. The greater the distance from awe at the impenetrability of divine reality, which is essentially proper to religious experience, the stronger the temptation to resort to linguistic 'conceptualism' and to fall victim to the erroneous conviction that the reality of the divine mystery can be 'grasped' or 'comprehended' by means of concepts. The category of experience (*anubhava*), on the other hand, plays a major part in Asian Christian theology. The emphasis on the category of experience is not intended primarily as an antithesis to the epistemic aspect of divine revelation, that is, to the aspect subject to the validation of cognition. It has evolved instead on the basis of a deeply-rooted tradition of meditation and immersion in the mystery of ultimate reality. The experience of 'enlightenment' or 'illumination' (*satori* or *samadhi*) conduces more intensely to silence than it calls for expression. The most profound spiritual experience shuns hasty communication and favours discretion.

In developing their own Asian approach, Asian Christian theologians see themselves in a totally new situation in the history of the Church and of theology, when they come to grips with what seem to them most urgent questions about the significance of Jesus Christ in religiously pluralistic Asian societies, and when they inquire into the theological significance of other religions and their founders (to name only the central questions of an Asian theology). Accordingly, they are not prepared to accept the admonition that they should look only to traditional theological methodology for the solution of these problems. Their approach to encounters with other religions and cultures is fundamentally different from that of Western theology, which met these religions outwardly in order to plumb, or rather generally to deny, their theological and salvation-historical riches. Asian theologians start from 'within', by claiming religious and cultural traditions as their own heritage and trying to make them fruitful. Accordingly, Asian Christian theologians look to the cultural and religious traditions of Asia as a *locus theologicus*, that is, as a source for their own practice of theology alongside the traditional sources of Scripture, tradition and magisterium. In the search for an Asian theological methodology, forms of interpretation and exegesis of sacred scriptures in Buddhism, Hinduism, Confucianism, Taoism and Islam are investigated to see if they can yield elements that will be of value in biblical hermeneutics and exegesis. The use and function of symbols, narratives and myths in Asian religious traditions offer many starting-points that enable Asian theologians to overcome any fixation on the philosophico-dogmatic formulations of Western theology. Their many years of experience as a religious minority compelled to live and assert themselves within the cultural and religious diversity of Asia leads Asian theologians to accept religious pluralism primarily as a reality. But at the same time they also try to elicit the deeper theological meaning that lies within it, and to draw on it for the benefit of their theological and ecclesial understanding of their own situation. People in Asia are used to living in a culturally and religiously diverse world to be treated with tolerance and where contradictions must be endured. But monoculturally conditioned European theologians and church leaders find it difficult to accept a plurality of ideologies and religions. Asian Christian theologians tend to treat differences in languages, cultures and hermeneutics within Asia more sympathetically and realistically than is the case in Western theology. Their own harsh experience has shown them only too well that there are limits to the 'translatability' of certain terminologies and terms, not because the translators are incompetent, but because the structures of certain Asian languages resist an adequate translation of many concepts originating in the Graeco-Roman philosophical tradition.[2]

Their experiences of interreligious dialogue lead Asian theologians to try to develop a 'dialogal language'. They remark that from a long way back the Church and theology have used various language-games which, unfortunately, when invoked in contacts with those outside the Church, were, and still are, applied with minimal attention to nuance and sensitivity. There is liturgical language, in which adoration, praise, thanks, and intercession are addressed directly to God. Then there is dogmatic language, which uses philosophical terminology to present truths of Christian doctrine as distinguished from deviant formulations. Apologetical language defends Christian doctrine from attacks from without. Until now there has been a sad lack of the language-game of dialogal discourse urgently called for by new theological insights. This absence is a negative feature of dialogue with adherents of other religions, where language is applied that is intended for use in the Church, and contains meaningful denominational expressions which appear overpowering and intrusive in dialogue intended for 'outsiders'. Language appropriate for dialogue requires sensitivity and an open attitude to others, as well as an effort to be inclusive rather than exclusive, without any underlying attempt to brainwash others or to induce them to adopt one's own way of thinking and behaviour.

II Contentious theological questions between Asian theologians and Rome

I do not intend to go into the details of individual cases of Asian theologians who have been criticized and censured by the Roman magisterium. I shall merely cite a few memorable examples. They include the censure of the writings of the Indian Jesuit Anthony de Mello (1931–87), which was published by the Congregation for the Doctrine of the Faith in June 1989, two years after his death. The 1997 excommunication of the Sri Lankan theologian Tissa Balasuriya OMI received worldwide attention.[3] Less coverage was given to the case of the Korean theologian Jemin Ri. In a book published in 1995,[4] he sharply criticized the condition of the Korean church and revealed a number of grievances of the Korean clergy. The Catholic Bishops' Conference reacted by ordering a judicial inquiry directed against Jemin Ri and relegated the case to Rome, which promptly punished him by withdrawing his licence to teach. There was also much concern about the proceedings against Jacques Dupuis SJ, whose book *Towards a Christian Theology of Religious Pluralism* was censured by the Congregation for the Doctrine of Faith in October 1999 on account of views on Christology that were deemed to deviate from the teaching of the Church. After lengthy discussions during which Dupuis tried to show that the accusations levelled against him were unjustifiable, the book was not condemned but in a notification issued by the Congregation in January

2001 the author was merely required to indicate in any new edition that the views expressed in his book did not wholly accord with the teaching of the Church.

I shall now concentrate on a summary of the critical points raised against Asian theology by the Roman magisterium. No use was made subsequently of the great opportunity that might have been seized after the rediscovery of episcopal collegiality at the Second Vatican Council, and the few approaches to more intensive cooperation between bishops and the Curia were scaled down once again. As with the foundation of the Latin American Bishops' Conference CELAM in 1968, in the case of the foundation of the Association of Asian Bishops' Conferences (FABC) in 1971, the central Roman authority was not slow to communicate its general reserve about continental bishops' conferences. The Roman view was that continental bishops' conferences could be of use in matters of coordination and organization, but the authorities were more sceptical about any activities in the theological sector that might reach beyond those benefits. These general reservations about any form of intermediate instances between the local bishops and the central Roman authority meant that the central magisterium of the Church scarcely appreciated the abundant contributions to central questions of interreligious dialogue, the theology of religions, theological methodology, the social apostolate and the theology of the laity, that were developed and documented in the FABC seminar programmes over so many years. The potential outcomes of the continental bishops' conferences held in the period between 1994 and 1999 were heavily restricted by the set of planning rules imposed on them in advance by Rome, which determined the production of the preparatory documents, the timetable and programme, and the scope of addresses.[5] This was very clearly evident in the case of the special synod of Asian bishops in 1998, for which the Roman authorities ordained the main lines of its preparation (*Lineamenta, Instrumentum Laboris*) and the proceedings, all the way to the publication of the results, whereas contributions from the local Asian churches played no more than a subordinate role. It is indicative that the answer to the *Lineamenta* from the Japanese bishops, who sent their own draft and explained that they found the questions sent by Rome irrelevant in their case, was received in Rome with astonishment and displeasure.[6]

In respect of Asian theology the Roman authorities advance a general criticism of the claim of Asian theologians that they intend to develop new forms of a theology in its own right, which are distinct from traditional

Western theology with regard to both methodology and content. The theological commission of the FABC has presented fundamental contributions towards an Asian theology in several documents under the guiding theme of a 'theology of harmony'.[7] But the magisterium proffers the general objection to Asian theologians that they postulate a radical contrast between the 'logical thinking of the West' and the 'symbolic thinking of the East', intimating that the latter is better able to uphold the mystery of divine reality, which has been neglected in Western theology with its unilateral focus on rational knowledge. This blanket criticism overlooks the fact that Asian theologians wish to invoke and apply fruitfully in Christian theology new insights of respect for that mystery developed from Asian traditions, without excluding recourse to reason. There is no reason why the reticence expressed in Asian theology about too great a degree of rationalization should not also be understood and accepted beyond Asian theology as enriching theology and not endangering it.

Another critical point concerns the interest of Asian theologians in trying to extend the conventional sources of theology (Scripture, tradition and the magisterium) to accommodate philosophical and theological traditions of Asian countries, if not as sources then as theological resources. But the magisterium has rejected the valuation of written tradition in Asian religions as 'sacred scriptures', as represented by some Asian theologians, as irreconcilable with the Church's understanding of revelation. The limited use of these scriptures in the Christian liturgy, as attempted in India, was firmly censured.[8]

In 1989, in a communication entitled *Some Aspects of Christian Meditation*, the Congregation for the Doctrine of the Faith criticized the adoption by Western churches of eastern meditation techniques. There were objections to some of these methods of meditation as impersonal techniques producing automatic results that imprison devout practitioners in a purely inward spiritualism, and do not enable them to open themselves up freely to the transcendent God (No. 3). Considering Asian religiousness and mysticism, the document makes a sharp distinction between an 'Asian identity mysticism' and the 'Christian mysticism of personal love'. In this connection the document also criticized the use of a 'negative theology' which 'denies that the things of this world can offer indications leading to God's infinity' (No. 13).[9] That viewpoint would contradict the Church's pronouncement that God's redemptive mystery has been fully and completely revealed in Jesus Christ (DJ 6). Admittedly the document does concede that meditation practices drawn from leading eastern religions 'prove attractive to directionless people today and in the midst of external turmoil can be appropriate aids to a relaxed stance before God' (No. 28). This presentation turns these forms of meditation into more properly esoteric practices, that might perhaps prove helpful for those without any religious affiliation, but cannot constitute a serious alternative for believing Christians. The basic tenor of the document is that the Christian tradition of meditation and prayer is perfect and does not need to be supplemented or enriched by Asian tradition. At the time of this communication, the negative statements of the Congregation for the Doctrine of the Faith about Asian forms of meditation were strongly contradicted by Asian theologians, and were also found frustrating by those in the West who had found their spiritual path by using these methods of meditation.[10]

Dominus Jesus, the 6 August 2000 document of the Congregation for the Doctrine of the Faith is highly significant with regard to the Roman magisterium's criticism of theologian positions represented by Asian theologians.[11] This document brings together central objections to the work of Asian theologians. Asian theologians are accused not only of treating religious pluralism, which is particularly evident in Asia, as a fact (*de facto*), but of a readiness to accept and recognize it as legitimate or lawful (*de iure*) (DJ 4). From the Roman viewpoint, this is tantamount at the very least to an impermissible diminution of the missionary commission to proclaim the Gospel of Jesus Christ to all humankind. The attitude towards other religions that is widespread among Asian theologians, treating them as companions on the same road, entering into dialogue with them, and working together to achieve a more human world, is condemned as a relativist mentality irreconcilable with Catholic tradition and the faith of the Church (DJ 5). This attitude is said to have induced Asian theologians to represent positions that deviate from ecclesiastical tradition and the magisterium in their pronouncements on the person and mission of Jesus Christ, the redemptive significance of other religions, the value and status of the sacred writings of those religions, and the role of their founders. A further criticism is that the concept of the Kingdom of God developed by Asian theologians turns it by anthropocentric constriction into a purely mundane and secularized reality in which the struggle for socio-economic, political and cultural liberation is of vital importance, but is closed to transcendent implications (RM 17 und DJ 4). Another objection is that Asian theologians see the Kingdom of God as a reality detached from the

Church. It is also objected that the statement that God's redemptive activity is reflected in the entire reality of creation, and in the multiplicity of cultures and religions, would tend to obscure and devalue the redemptive activity of Jesus Christ, which finds its eschatological fulfilment in the Church as the sacrament of salvation. Another condemnation is directed against the playing off of a 'theocentricity' based on the doctrine of the Kingdom of God against the kind of 'ecclesiocentricity' of the kind put forward by theologians who give a unilateral emphasis to the Kingdom of God (DJ 19 with reference to RM 17), which the Asians suggest is erroneous.

The criticism of the Christological contributions of Asian theologians by the Roman magisterium is directed against the notion of a distinction between the historical Jesus and the eschatological Logos.[12] Raimon Panikkar made this distinction when he said that Jesus of Nazareth is indeed Christ, but that Christ is more than the historical Jesus.[13] These statements, which have been made in similar terms by other Asian theologians, certainly do not intend any separation between Jesus of Nazareth and the Logos (Messiah). The purpose of these Christological contributions is rather to distinguish between the functions and redemptive significance of the earthly life of Jesus Christ and the redemption already achieved with him, and the still outstanding fulfilment at the end of all the ages. *Dominus Jesus*, without citing specific names, accuses Asian theologians of effecting a 'metaphysical deflation of the event which is the incarnation of the eternal Logos in time', which so attenuates it as to make it 'no more than a mere manifestation of God in history' (DJ 4). Then Jesus Christ would become a certainly unique yet limited historical figure, and one in whom the divine would have been revealed not absolutely but restrictively, so that he becomes a mere complement to other salvific figures (DJ 9). Similarly, in an intervention at the seventh plenary assembly of the FABC in Bangkok in January 2000, Cardinal Jozef Tomko, the then Prefect of the Congregation for the Doctrine of Faith, reproached Asian theologians for representing a 'weak Christology', since they placed Jesus Christ on the same footing as the sacred figures of other religions, and thereby watered down the uniqueness and absolute nature of God's revelation in Jesus.

A constantly recurrent objection raised against Asian theologians is that they have been untrue to Christ's missionary purpose by according interreligious dialogue the primacy over missionary endeavours. The far too great immediacy of the religious teachings and practices of meditation and prayer of the Eastern religions is said to have led to a reduction or partial obscuring of Christian identity among theologians, bishops and priests, and even more emphatically among laypeople. Out of fear of proselytism (so the objections say), they might think that their duty of mission was satisfied if they helped others to be more human and to persist in the lines of their own religious traditions.[14] The Roman authorities have viewed Asian theologians as open to the danger of a growing syncretism that could lead to a perilous relativism, spreading from Asia to infect the 'old' churches of the West.[15] In its 'Theses on Interreligious Dialogue', the FABC theological advisory commission confirmed that religions undergoing a process of renewal and revitalization were in a situation that was totally novel in the history of the Church, where it was no longer a matter of the Church's relation to other cultures and religions, but of redefining the place and role of the Church in a religiously and culturally pluralistic world. In the process they emphasized the fact that dialogue and mission were integral, dialectical and complementary dimensions of the Church's one mission of evangelization. Asian theologians have affirmed that the universal presence and operation of the Spirit are evident in religions. Consequently these religions represent positive elements in the divine plan of salvation, and since God has made himself known in their sacred Scriptures, they contain a message for all humanity.[16]

III Confirmation of unity and theological pluralism in the Church

There is a fundamental temptation within the Church, while making justified and necessary efforts to ensure the unity of the Church, to insist on notional uniformity with regard to all major truths of faith. But this is a betrayal of the theological insight that every conceptual dogmatic formulation is no more than an inadequate attempt to express the mystery of God and Jesus Christ (Eph 3.18) analogically in different language-games. Accordingly, a universal Church domiciled in many cultures has to allow a multiplicity of different paradigms to enjoy equal rights. In order to put this into practice, a form of dialogue within the Church is required that guarantees intercommunication between the various paradigms. This calls for expert interpreters who are well-acquainted with numerous paradigms and, as universal ecclesiastical mediators – like missionary forces in the world Church drawn from all the churches – work to make unity in multiplicity a living reality. Aloysius Pieris SJ has remarked that most Asian theologians have learned how to do theology in several languages and thought-patterns, whereas western theology for the most part knows only one way of thinking and one linguistic form and still treats this combination as universally binding.[17] There is a tension between the great value and great task of ensuring unity in the universal Church on the one hand, and affirming pluralism in theology on the other hand. This tension necessarily arises from the fact that the Christian message is proclaimed in different cultural, religious and anthropological contexts. Ultimately, surrendering to the temptation of trying to combine these various theological projects in a new synthesis all over again would mean saying goodbye to any genuine pluralism. All those who affirm that theological pluralism is essential and enriching for an understanding of the mystery of Jesus Christ will and must be able to tolerate the (necessary) existence of lasting difficulties in understanding between different theological projections. Not to allow this diversity to flourish, but to try to restrain it, and ultimately to eradicate it for the sake of a single unified theology, would mean reviving the danger of a new Rites Controversy, with all the negative consequences that history tells us would flow from that.[18]

Translated by J. G. Cumming

Notes

1. J. Gnanapirragasam & F. Wilfred (eds), *Being Church in Asia: Theological Advisory Commission Documents, 1986–1992*, Manila, 1994.
2. This makes the strong criticism emanating from Asian local churches comprehensible when they object to the practice of Roman authorities of checking and approving translations of liturgical texts into any language. They also criticize the transplantation of gestures, postures and other liturgical incidentals with Graeco-Roman antecedents, even though they are found incomprehensible or annoying in Asia and in Africa.
3. Cf. G. Evers, 'Kontextuelle Theologie in Asien. Zur Exkommunikation Tissa Balasuriyas', *StdZ* 122 (1997), 3pp. 74–86; *id*. 'The Excommunication of Tissa Balasuriya: A Warning to Asian Theologians?', *Jeevadhara* 27 (1997), No. 159, pp. 212–30.
4. Jemin Ri, *The Church – Casta Meretrix: The Second Vatican Council and the Korean Church*, Waegwan, 1995.
5. G. Evers, 'The Continental Bishops' Synods – Lost Chance or New Beginning?', *Jeevadhara* 30 (2000), No. 177, pp. 313–29.
6. G. Evers, 'Die Sonderversammlung der Bischofssynode für Asien', *Die Katholischen Missionen* 117 (1998), pp. 118–9; *id*., 'Die asiatischen Bischöfe auf ihrer Synode', in: *Herder Korrespondenz* 52 (1998), pp. 356–61.

7. 'Asian Perspectives on Harmony', in: *For All the Peoples of Asia*, vol. II, Manila, 1997, pp. 229–98.
8. Criticism of the assumption that the Scriptures of other religions 'could be inspired by the Holy Spirit' is to be found, e. g., in *Dominus Jesus*, No. 8.
9. The same objection also appears later in *Dominus Jesus*, when Asian theologians are criticized for their fundamental questioning of the possibility that divine truths can be adequately and authentically reproduced in human language and philosophical terminology.
10. Cf. A. Samy, *Vidyajyoti* 54 (1990) 3, pp. 155–63; S. Painadath, *Vidyajyoti* 54, 3, pp. 387–99.
11. G. Evers, '"Dominus Jesus" und die Theologie in Asien', in: *Herder Korrespondenz* 54 (2000), pp. 618–22; *id.*, 'Recognize the Creativity of the Local Churches', *Jeevadhara* XXXI, No. 183, pp. 187–92.
12. See, e. g., John Paul II in *Redemptoris Missio* No. 6, and also in the declaration of the Congregation for the Doctrine of Faith, *Dominus Jesus*, No. 4.
13. The original English text reads thus: 'Jesus is the Christ, but Christ is more than Jesus'.
14. See, e. g., *Redemptoris Missio*, No. 46.
15. Cf. P. Mujzes & L.Swidler (eds), *Christian Mission and Interreligious Dialogue*, New York, n. d., pp. 236–62.
16. J. Gnanapiragasam & F. Wilfred (eds), *Being Church in Asia*, Manila, 1994, pp. 8, 20.
17. Cf. A. Pieris, 'Christologie in Asien. Eine Antwort an Felipe Gomez', in: *id.*, *Feuer und Wasser*, Freiburg im Breisgau,1994, pp. 35–49.
18. Karl Rahner referred to this danger in one of his last publications. Cf. K. Rahner, 'Ritenstreit: Neue Aufgabe für die Kirche', in: *Schriften zur Theologie* XVI, Freiburg im Breisgau, 1984, pp. 178–84. See also the similar reference by Felix Wilfred, 'Grundlegende Probleme einer asiatischen Theologie', *Herder Korrespondenz* 53 (1999), pp. 26–33.

Church, Theology and Magisterium in Latin America: Unnecessary Conflicts and Inevitable Tensions

AGENOR BRIGHENTI

The brief history of Latin American theology, an adventure still in progress, is marked by important contributions to the Church's long theological tradition, but also by many wounds inflicted by misunderstandings, bans, investigations and punishments of theologians. Given the current arrangements in the Church, this is hardly a surprise, since our Latin American theological tradition, starting from the premises of modern civilized culture, particularly the emancipation of practical reason achieved through the second Enlightenment, has been marked by a militantly prophetic approach, which included the Church among its objects.

The reasons for the frequent conflicts between the magisterium and theologians, especially with particular bishops, are varied. Basically they arise from three factors, deriving from an internal tension inherent in theology itself. This consists in theology's three dimensions, both difficult to reconcile and at the same time inseparable or in strict dialectical relation.[1] The first has to do with the scientific character of theology, a consequence of the cognitive dimension of faith, which necessarily results in critical thought. The second is connected with its claim to truth, something common to all science, within the characteristics of language, which is always context-based and limited, which makes theology a human product and therefore knowledge 'about' the Absolute rather than absolute knowledge. The third factor is the ecclesial dimension of Christian faith, which makes the authenticity of a theology dependent on its ecclesial character, which inevitably gives rise to tensions between the 'uncritical faith' of most Christians, the 'critical faith' of professional theologians and the 'vigilant faith' of the magisterium.

The conflicts provoked by this way of doing theology in society and the institution of the Church should make it unnecessary to say that they result from its challenging attitude. This attitude has profound consequences for Christianity, especially for the Catholic Church, because it produces a new approach to the mission of evangelization, of theology, for the way the magisterium is exercised, and so on. It is a way of doing theology that is significantly destabilizing of the premises that have historically underpinned the conception of unity in faith and in the Church, and of the relationship between theology and science, between the social actions of the Church and theological reflection, and between theologians and the episcopal college. It subverts the traditional way of understanding the universality of the Church and its truth criteria, presenting the challenge of an exercise of unity that is not only decentralized but also de-concentrated and arguing for a truth that is less epistemological and more ontological, and one also subjected to the test of action.

I Notes from an adventure still in progress

Before examining the reasons for the conflicts between theologians and the magisterium in Latin America, as it is a situation that also gives theology 'pause for thought', let us review some of these frictions, with an eye to the following section. Contrary to what is widely thought, Latin American theology is not dead, as can be seen by the many conflicts still alive in both society and Church. In society there are the martyrs, past and present. In the Church, apart from the list of theologians banned from many Church activities or whose associations are ignored by Church authorities, there was their absence from events such as the Fifth General Conference of Latin American and Caribbean Bishops, held in Aparecida (Brazil) in 2007. A similar ban operated at the previous two conferences, Puebla (1979) and Santo Domingo (1992).

1 An unconventional theology

To clarify the difficult relationship between the magisterium and theology in Latin America, it may be useful to summarize the particular character of our theological method. At the end of the 1960s in Latin America an 'unconventional' way of doing theology exploded on to the stage that came to be labelled 'liberation theology'. It was unconventional because, rather than the result of a carefully designed plan, it arose out of the need to consider, in the light of faith, the pressing problems of responsible Church action, as a requirement of bringing together the living consciousness of the Church and theological reflection. As a result, the subject of this work came to be defined by the urgent pastoral challenges faced by Church communities, living both realistically and prophetically in a harsh society.

Liberation theology was developed under very unfavourable conditions. It did not have the time needed to mature naturally. It was put together under pressure from within and without, and was forced to bear fruit prematurely. It emerged, grew and developed in little less than ten years, specifically between the conferences of Medellín (1968) and Puebla (1979).[2] In the space of a decade in the 1970s, it developed not merely its method, its identity, but even an ecclesiology and a Christology designed to illuminate and interpret the new faith situation of the Church in Latin America and the Caribbean.[3] They were times of intense creativity, followed by times of difficulty, whether from attempts by particular Church authorities to crush it or from profound internal turbulences. Internally, one difficult moment was the move from 'the theology of liberation' to 'theologies of liberation', that is, from a common, converging intuition that was at the root of liberation theology to a gradual diversification of outlooks, as a result of historical experiences, regional or cultural differences, but above all of the need to widen the concept of 'poverty'. It was then that feminist theology, black theology, indigenous theology and eco-theology emerged.

2 Ecclesiastical pressure

Both theologians and sectors of the Church associated with liberation theology have been and continue to be subject to pressure, both secular and ecclesiastical. Nevertheless, however harsh may have been the pressures from outside the Church, the most painful have come, and continue to come, from within.

While the teaching of Medellín was still in the process of being absorbed, the close collaboration between bishops and theologians received its first blow from the strategy adopted by CELAM (the Latin American Episcopal Council) at its ordinary assembly in Sucre (Bolivia) in 1972.[4] The four theological institutes (catechetics in Chile and in Manizales, Colombia, pastoral theology in Quito, Ecuador, and liturgy in Medellín, Colombia) were centralized in Colombia, and theologians in the Latin

American tradition were prevented from teaching there. The Latin American Conference of Religious (CLAR) was forbidden to implement its catechetical programme 'Word and Life' (*Palabra y Vida*) and subsequently suffered Vatican intervention with the imposition of an outside executive hostile to the liberationist perspective. At Puebla, Santo Domingo and even at the recent Aparecida conference, theologians from the Latin American perspective were excluded.

More publicly, investigations were opened into the three main pillars of this new theological edifice – Gustavo Gutiérrez, Leonardo Boff and Jon Sobrino – that resulted in the punishment of Boff and a formal warning to Sobrino, this last on the eve of the Aparecida conference. This list could go on, with Ivone Gebara, José María Vígil and others. More covertly, but in an equally arbitrary manner, there now came a series of bans on theologians from attending theological conferences and some church events, and others were prevented from lecturing in universities or theological institutes.

In spite of this, to counteract the fragmentation, many theological associations were now founded, some of them, such as that in Brazil, now over 30 years old, with annual conferences and significant academic work and publications. On the other hand, following the example of some Roman bodies, many bishops' conferences now created their own commissions for the Doctrine of the Faith, appointing to them Church theologians unconnected with the existing associations. Part of the same movement of creating a distance between themselves and modern critical theological analysis is the gradual transfer of theology courses designed for candidates for ordination from universities to seminaries. We are seeing the return of an ecclesiastical theology to the detriment of an ecclesial one, in touch with the great challenges of our time, especially the cause of the poorest and most excluded.

II The inevitable tension between Church, theology and the magisterium

Clashes between bishops and theologians are totally unnecessary and avoidable since they result largely either from defective theological method or personal or institutional limitations. Nevertheless it is necessary to bear in mind that, with the greatest possible charity and respect for differences, there are inevitable and salutary tensions inherent in the relationship between theology and magisterium. Clashes are impoverishing, but conflicts are enriching. The magisterium too needs research, debate and dialogue, needs to build consensus between different positions, including being able to respect dissent while expressing disagreement. Here Augustine's principle applies: 'In essentials unity, in what is secondary freedom and in all things charity.'

At the beginning of this article I mentioned underlying reasons for the friction between magisterium and theology, deriving from an internal tension inherent in theology itself as a result of the interrelationship of the three dimensions of theology: the cognitive dimension of faith, faith as human experience, and the ecclesial dimension of faith. I now want to look briefly at each of these.

1   Theology and the cognitive dimension of faith

Theology is not an act of reason, but it is nonetheless a reasonable act, since faith has a cognitive dimension. The task of theology is to give an account of Christian hope to those who ask for one. Here a particular point of tension within theology itself has to do with the type of reason that underpins it, pre-modern rationality or modern rationality. If theology wants to be a science, in the sense of an academic discipline, it must start from the basis of modern rationality. While it has its autonomy, it is not dispensed from appearing, together with the other academic disciplines, before what A. Gesché has called 'the court of reason'.[5] It also needs to ask itself what conditions have to be met for an argument to be scientific. 'Weberian disenchantment' has exposed as an illusion the claim to total objectivity, dominant for a long time within logical positivism. So have the physical sciences and mathematics freed us from subjectivity? Marx warned that if the subject's vision coincides with its object, the science is empty. The 'masters of suspicion', Marx, Nietzsche and Freud, exposed the limits of scientific reasoning. Kant, and more recently Popper, revealed the pre-scientific premises inherent in the methodology of all the sciences, exposing them to a 'critical rationalism' based on the realization that at the beginning of scientific activity there is what Hans Küng has called an 'irrational faith' in reason.

Alongside the inevitable presuppositions inherent in the method of any science, there is also the contingent nature of all scientific discourse. As shown by Dilthey and Gadamer in modern hermeneutics, and more recently by Thomas Kuhn and Michel Foucault, there is always the need for a general theory of society to validate scientific statements.[6] Therefore the unity of the sciences is only guaranteed by the communication between them, in the perspective of what Jürgen Habermas called 'communicative reason'.[7]

The consequences of this for theology are clear: it too is a human product, knowledge 'of' the Absolute and not absolute knowledge (*sacra theologia*). If this is the case, the magisterium cannot ask of theologians what they cannot give. It must recognize and respect science. And theologians need to proceed with scientific humility and intellectual honesty. In this connection, since science is carried out in the academy, it must be an anomaly for a theologian to require the *nihil obstat* of the magisterium to do theology in the Church's academies.

2 Theology and faith as human experience

Strictly speaking, the object of theology is not God, but the human experience of faith in God. Accordingly, theology's first step must be to enquire into the basis of the faith experience and whether this can be explained rationally. On this point Augustine made an important distinction between *fides qua* (the human being's unconditional openness to God, which is a gift from God himself, the faith by which one believes, the assent to a reality that is given to one, and *fides quae* (the propositions formulated about the act of faith, the faith to which credence is given, the formulations of the contents of faith.[8]

This distinction is important both for theology and for the magisterium, because it establishes two levels of truth, *objectifying truth* (one-dimensional, God himself, unattainable by scientific discourse) and *relational truth* (pluri-dimensional, the experience of encounter with God, the field of scientific truth). If this is the case, the object of theology is not God, but the human faith experience of encounter with God, or in other words propositions about God. Similarly, for the magisterium the question arises whether dogmas are 'objects' of faith or faith 'responses'. In pre-modern theology, without an awareness of all the limitations of scientific reasoning, it was thought that dogmas did no more than 'expound' the apostolic faith found in the Gospels, with no 'cultural accretions'. But Yves Congar showed that the anti-modern popes, starting with Gregory XVI's *Mirari vos* (1832), did theology, indeed a specific, limited theology. Believing honestly that they were defending the faith, they used all the means at their disposal to defend a specific culture.[9]

In *Donum Veritatis* (1990),[10] there are still remnants of this position in the claim that the nature of theology is defined by the 'object ... given by Revelation, handed on and interpreted in the Church under the authority of the magisterium, and received by faith'.[11] Faith here is not an immediate correlate of revelation, but an acceptance that comes after a process of interpretation authenticated by the magisterium. It is as though magisterium and revelation formed a single block and were a process prior to or taking precedence over the Church's faith. But the magisterium that interprets and transmits the faith can never replace the experience of the mystery, the closeness of God. Faith is not a mere intellectual assent to particular dogmatic formulae.

As has been shown, on the one hand the magisterium too has its limitations, its obligations, and its mission is not free from risk, though the fragility does not remove its authority, provided that it is willing to recognize its limitations. On the other hand, the conclusions of theology are always provisional because they are always approximations to Christian faith, because of the limitations of its research instruments. This is the origin of the constant plea to theologians 'to serve human beings in their thirst for total, ultimate and definitive truths', made by John Paul II in an address to theologians in Salamanca.[12]

3 The ecclesial dimension of theology

It is in the relation between theology and the Church that we find the sore point of the tension between magisterium and theology. The theologian's vocation is not a concession from the magisterium or derived from it, but is rooted in the ecclesial community's faith experience. This was clear for Latin American theology from the very beginning: the life of the ecclesial community is the 'natural home' of theology. This is an assertion not only that theology is inseparable from the living consciousness of the Church, but also a corresponding conviction that the life and experience of an ecclesial faith precede theology. Theology is always a 'second stage', a 'critical reflection on practise in the light of faith', as Gustavo Gutiérrez put it[13]: the effort to conceptualize experience lived in faith, the theoretical phase in the life and action of the Church. Because of this Latin American theology is an original contextual theology, not necessarily because of its method and still less because of its end results, but above all because of the ecclesial experience that sustains it. The essence of this theological paradigm is not theology, but the types of transformative action it generates, the incarnate experience of faith. It is from these that theology emerges as the attempt to understand faith, in a deliberate, intentional and reflex process *in*, *out of* and *for* the context of this faith experience. Its 'particularity' is not in its theology as such, nor its semantics, much less its syntax, but in the ecclesial experience from which it lives and for which it seeks to point ways forward that offer a response to specific challenges. In the last resort the new feature Latin American theology has introduced to other theologies is a change of place and function.

But the difficulties in the relationship between theologians and bishops, from the Latin America viewpoint, start from the ambiguities of the term 'Church' in the documents of the magisterium. Sometimes it means just the hierarchy. At others, while the phrase 'the universal Church' is used, in practice the reference is to the Latin Church. At root are at least two underlying modes of relationship between the magisterium and theology, deriving from two opposing models of ecclesiology.

4 The dependency relationship of a pre-conciliar ecclesiology

In the period before Vatican II, until Pius XII's Apostolic Constitution *Sedes sapientiae*, the dominant model of ecclesiology was that of the twelfth century, when law became a key element in the unity and cohesion of the Church.[14] For Pius X, for example, the Church is an unequal society, formed by two types of Christians, shepherds and sheep. The shepherds have all the rights and authority of initiative and leadership. The mass of the sheep have only to obey and meekly follow the hierarchy. The Pope is considered the direct source of all jurisdictional power.

In this model theology is a derivative function, dependent on the hierarchy, in the last analysis on the magisterium of the Pope himself. Consequently its conclusions do not have the same authentic character as those of the magisterium. There is no room for any possibility of autonomy for theology, even though it is recognized as a science. In *Sedes sapientiae* Pius XII states that 'since the deposit of revelation was entrusted exclusively to the Church's magisterium for authentic interpretation', and the magisterium is competent to do this 'following the sense and mind of the Church itself', theologians are under notice that 'they exercise their ministry, not in their own name or in their own right, but in the name and by the authority of the supreme magisterium, and therefore under its vigilance and control. From this magisterium they receive a sort of canonical office'. Accordingly, 'theologians are given teaching authority, not to share with their students their private opinions, but to impart to them the tried and tested teachings of the Church'.[15] Accordingly, as Pius XII had said in *Humanae Generis*, 'this Sacred Magisterium should be ... an immediate, a universal norm of truth for any theologian',[16] not only *ex cathedra* definitions, but 'constitutions, decrees of the Holy See' 'encyclicals of the Roman Pontiffs' and 'more recent constitutions and decrees'.[17]

Within these parameters there is no room at all for charism, only for the institution. Theology does not meet the basic conditions to be considered a scientific discipline, because in fact for this type of Church there is no place for critical reflection or even a *sensus fidei* or *sensus fidelium*. The function of theology is to repeat what the magisterium says. In fact, there is no trust in modern science, especially in modern instruments of research, which are suspect of subjectivism, in contrast to the scholastic tradition, which is held to be objective, as Pius XI testifies: 'The characteristic of Thomism is that it is above all objective...mental constructions that correspond to the reality of things'.[18] This is no longer theology, but philosophy, and a dubious philosophy.

5 The relationship in the ecclesiology of Vatican II

The Second Vatican Council overturned the dominant medieval ecclesiology, conceiving the Church as the People of God, within which the hierarchy has a more functional and service role than necessarily one of power. The Pope is placed within the episcopal college, and the source of unity in the Church is the Holy Spirit, who dispenses the diversity of gifts.

In the model of relationship between magisterium and theologians implicit in the ecclesiology of Vatican II, the ecclesial nature of theology acquires a different sense. The ministry of the theologian, a gift of the Spirit, is a function within the ecclesial community as a whole as a service for the good of the whole Church. In this respect, more in harmony with Vatican II's ecclesiology than *Donum Veritatis* is an address by John Paul II, given to scientists and university students in Cologne Cathedral on 15 November 1980.[19] The address starts with Albert the Great, for whom science is absolutely free and has only one rule, truth. And, moreover, theology as a science is included without restriction among sciences in general, with the same freedom and the same limitations as all sciences. Albert stressed that philosophy and theology 'are limited efforts' that can only explore truth 'within an open system of complementary items of knowledge. And, along with freedom, he also recognizes the provisional nature of theology's results and the impossibility of giving definitive answers. Consequently science, including theology, 'must be open, in fact it must also be multiform'.

On the basis of these premises, the Pope in Cologne, at the beginning of his pontificate, insisted that: 'The Church wants independent theological research, which is not identified with the ecclesiastical magisterium, but which knows it is committed with regard to it in common service of the truth of faith and the People of God' (par. 5). According to the Pope, conflicts and tensions between theology and the magisterium, such as those that occur between the Church and science, can be the result of caprice, which is always harmful, but there is a salutary and inevitable tension that derives from the limits of reason and of the methods available. Theology is not a 'delegated function' dependent on the magisterium, but a science free to apply its methods and analyses, although it always has to bear in mind the faith lived by the community of the faithful. Accordingly, 'the theologian teaches in the name of and by virtue of the mandate of the ecclesial faith community'. In the same perspective *Donum Veritatis* said: 'The canonical mission given by the pastor to the theologian does not mark the beginning of his charism, but only its official recognition, since charisms are given by the Holy Spirit.' For the Pope, fidelity to the witness of faith and to the magisterium do not 'divert theologians from their work or deprive them of their inalienable autonomy'.[20]

It is in this sense that Thomas Aquinas talked of two magisteria in the Church, the magisterium of the bishops and the magisterium of the theologians, obviously with different functions. It is for the theologian to make proposals to aid the understanding of faith, but these have to be submitted to the Church as a whole, for possible correction and expansion in a fraternal dialogue leading to a consensus of the whole faith community. In short, in the conditions of modern science, theology can only be fragmentary, plural and hypothetical. It is not theology that possesses the truth, but the truth that possesses it.

By way of conclusion

Given these two very different models of the relationship between theology and the magisterium, if the Vatican II model is the one presumed to be in force, why are there still attitudes of suspicion towards theologians and so many control measures applied to the institutions within which they work?

Leaving aside the misunderstandings resulting from personal whims and a sinful Church, and the natural tensions inherent in theology, the conflicts between magisterium and theologians in Latin America involve at least three fundamental issues. The first concerns the failure to take sufficiently into account the scientific character of theology, now that its methods are on a level with those of modern reasoning. To be a science of faith, it needs spaces of freedom and autonomy *vis-à-vis* the magisterium, and for its part the magisterium needs to be aware of the limitations of science, whose results are always provisional and always remain open to new approximations to a truth that infinitely surpasses it. There is circularity between truth and freedom. Truth sets us free, and freedom leads to truth. Any restriction on freedom distorts the truth. Repression defends its ideological version of the truth.

The second issue lies within the field of the theology of revelation. Revelation is often understood as a 'deposit' to be simply explained and transmitted by the magisterium, with the collaboration of theologians. On this point we need to bear in mind how the process of revelation occurs and the sense in which the Bible is the Word of God. We also need to be aware that the Church's role as the trustee of the fullness of revelation does not mean that this role is exclusive to her or that she has understood everything, especially when the truths of the faith reach us in a human way and within the conceptual limits of a particular period. As Augustine says: 'If you understand, it's not God.'

The third fundamental question is in the field of hermeneutics, which is a function of human beings' inherent desire to interpret the world. Reason is interpretative, since our knowledge of reality is inevitably marked by finite perspectives, situations and apprehensions of meaning. We do not possess any absolute knowledge because we have no privileged position that gives us access to reality in itself. All knowledge is an approximation to reality, mediated by language, which seeks to capture a reality that is fundamentally symbolic. In theology what we can have of the truth are formulations that are provisional, diverse and not necessarily false. What at first sight may appear false may be no more than a 'conflict of interpretations', something healthy for theology, since it must always remain 'fragmentary, plural and hypothetical'. As *Donum Veritatis* stresses, a greater approximation to the truth 'entails in essence an objective discussion, a fraternal dialogue, an openness and willingness to modify one's own opinions'.[21]

Translated by Francis McDonagh

1. Cf. Ricardo Franco, 'Teología y Magisterio: dos modelos de relación', *Estudios Eclesiásticos* 59 (1984), pp. 3–25, quotation from p. 3.
2. Cf. J. O. Beozzo, 'Medellín: vinte anos depois (1968–1988). Depoimentos a partir do Brasil', *REB* 192 (1988), pp. 771–805.
3. Cf. Carlos Palacio, 'Trinta anos de teologia na América Latina. Um depoimento', in Luís Carlos Susin (ed.), *O mar se abriu : Trinta anos de teologia na América Latina*, São Paulo, 2000, pp. 51–64.
4. On the about-turn in CELAM after the Sucre assembly of 1972, cf. F. Houtart, 'Le Conseil Épiscopal d'Amérique latine accentue son changement', *ICI* 481 (1975), pp. 10–24.
5. Cf. A. Gesché and Paul Scolas, *La foi dans le temps du risque*, Paris, 1997.
6. Cf. T. S. Kuhn, *The Structure of Scientific Revolutions*, Chicago & London, 1962, [3]1996.
7. Cf. J. Habermas, *The Theory of Communicative Action*. Vol. 1: *Reason and the rationalization of society*, Vol. 2: *Lifeworld and the system: a critique of functionalist reason*, London and Boston MA, 1984–7.
8. Cf. *De Trinitate* XXX, II, 5.
9. Cf. Y. Congar, 'Les théologiens et l'Église', in *Les quatre fleuves* 12, Paris, 1980, p. 11.
10. Congregation for the Doctrine of the Faith, 'Instruction *Donum Veritatis,* On the Ecclesial Vocation of the Theologian', 8, *AAS* 82 (1990), 1552–3.
11. Cf. Ricardo Antonich, 'El servicio intelectual a la verdad. Reflexiones en torno a la instrucción sobre la Vocación Eclesial del Teólogo', *Medellín* 65 (1991), pp. 113–29, quotation from p. 123.
12. Quoted by Ricardo Franco, 'Teología y Magisterio', *op. cit.* p. 12. English translation from *L'Osservatore Romano*.
13. This is the classic definition of the characteristic approach of Latin American theology, coined by Gustavo Gutiérrez, *A Theology of Liberation. History, Politics and Salvation*, rev. ed, London 2001. The book, originally published in 1971, was immediately translated into Italian (1972), English (1973), French (1974) and German (1975).
14. Y. Congar, *L'Église de St. Augustin à l'époque moderne*, Paris, 1970, p. 145.
15. *AAS* 48 (1956), p. 36
16. *AAS* 42 (1950), p. 567.
17. *Ibidem*, p. 567.
18. DS 2876.
19. This section relies largely on the summary made by Ricardo Franco from M. Seckler, *Im Spannungsfeld von Wissenschaft und Kirche*, Freiburg, Basle & Vienna, 1980, in 'Teología y Magisterio', *op. cit.*, pp. 19–20. English version from *L'Osservatore Romano*.
20. *Donum Veritatis*, 23.
21. *Donum Veritatis*, 11.

Magisterium and Theology: Principles and Facts

ANDRES TORRES QUEIRUGA

Vatican II laid foundations and opened doors. The very fact that it took place was a splendid exercise in new possibilities: collaboration between bishops and theologians was not easy to get going but it proved extremely fruitful. Without it the results of the Council would have been unthinkable; it was an exercise in Church fellowship, which made it possible to start a new ecclesiology. It resorted to original insights and practices and revived them for the present time after centuries – especially recent centuries – of institutional fossilization.

I Note on the Spanish situation

After the Council, the principles of a new relationship between the magisterium and theology were set up and ready to put into practice. But that was not easy: intellectual inertia and the instinctive dynamics of power played their part in certain unfortunate interventions, not only within the academy – such as the compromises that burdened many texts with ambiguity – but also from outside, such as the untimely *nota praevia* or the reserving of certain topics by the Pope in the face of the most universal of councils. From then on, until today, things have got worse, and the principles are in danger of being suffocated, weighed down by a tendency to deny them in practice – in the name of the Council.

In some countries like Spain this reaction has become much worse recently. After a period of definite advance – not without serious setbacks, such as the opposition to the Joint Assembly of Bishops and Priests (1971)[1] – after Cardinal Agravado ceased to be president of the CEE (Conferencia Episcopal Española = Catholic Spanish Bishops' Conference) there was a marked and increasing authoritarianism. Lately this has been aggravated by the predominance of a small group of theologians–disliked by some of the bishops and, it would seem, also by Rome. Through the Faith Commission this group of theologians has imposed an iron censorship on any proposal to modernize. Their censorship has very little theological weight and is clearly anti-Council. Theological works which appear in other European countries without hindrance are victims of its censorship. Even the Secretary of the Congregation for the Doctrine of the Faith, Monsignor Ladaria,[2] and the winner of the 2011 'Ratzinger Prize'[3] were attacked with serious accusations by members of this group. The recent case of the book *Jesús aproximación histórica* (2007) (ET: *Jesus. An Historical Approximation* (Convivium 2009) by J. A Pagola was the last straw. It involved his own bishop in the censorship who, after careful examination, expressly went along with it.

The damage to theological studies and the blatant loss of credibility for the Church are obvious consequences, whose seriousness it is hard to gauge. But this anomalous situation is also an exaggerated reflection of a general climate and what is really important is to analyse it.

II The Patristic 'Perichoresis' that is impossible today

Max Seckler aptly used this word to set the problem in its patristic context. Then the bishop was the teacher, the pastor was the theologian: in his person the two functions combined a living and fruitful *perichoresis* (circuminsession).[4] This confers a special and perpetual value upon his writings. But that time has passed and cultural change has made simple continuity impossible, as in fact it would now be a dead letter. In the religious field, as in all others, cultural differentiation imposes a clearer distinction of functions. The pastor can no longer fulfil the function of the theologian and likewise, the theologian must renounce his temptation to govern.[5]

It is not accidental that this differentiation took place in the Middle Ages, when with the full arrival of Aristotle and the foundation of the university, theology developed its status as a 'science'. From then on the Thomistic distinction between the *magisterium cathedrae pastoralis* (which 'commands and decides') and the *magisterium cathedrae magistralis* (which 'investigates and teaches') becomes a necessity.[6] The former *perichoresis* becomes impossible', but, of course, it should still 'give us something to think about'. Our task *today* is to set up a dialectic that keeps the fundamental continuity but respects the cultural difference.

Here, significantly – and perhaps uniquely in history – Benedict XVI clearly set out the distinction between the two magisteria in the prologue to the first volume of his Christology: 'Of course, I do not need to say explicitly that this book is in no way an act of the magisterium but simply the expression of my personal quest for "the Lord's face" (cf. Ps. 27:8). So anyone is free to contradict me. I only ask my readers' good will, without which no understanding is possible.' The pastor comes down from his throne and joins the theologians in the hall, in order to share in dialogue as one among equals.

However, the clarity of the principle is seldom carried out properly in practice. We can be certain that Pope Benedict will never deny the principle which he proclaimed with such clear courage. But we can't be as certain that it will be put into practice. His role as 'pope theologian', together with his specialization in Augustine and Bonaventure (who never accepted St Thomas's 'scientific' theology), has led in his long pastoral career – first as Prefect and then as Pope – to a style which tends to reassert the ancient *perichoresis*. And this then tends to merge the two magisteria, so that the 'scientific' value of his theology tends to clothe itself with the 'pastoral' authority of his ministry.

Indeed, it is difficult to deny that today there is an attempt to convert *his* theology into a norm for theology as a whole (this is more pronounced in certain doctrinaire proponents than in the pope himself). It is obvious that although the *Catechism of the Catholic Church* is not actually his own work, it is basically derived from his influence and inspiration. And, what is worse, this adds a second confusion of levels, by investing a 'catechetical' book with direct 'theological' authority. There are obvious intentions to do the same with his *Christology*, which, whatever its merits, still remains *one* Christology among a current flowering of other equally legitimate Christologies. The final danger, which can be seen in exaggerations such those mentioned above, would be a *confusion between faith and theology,* between radical Christian experience and a particular limited way of interpreting it.

This mixture of historical advance and a certain latent ambiguity also appears in the unprecedented and brave action of a pope who is capable of entering into public dialogue with non-believing philosophers and thinkers. For example, the encounter with Habermas was a pleasant surprise to all. However, here too the *current* ambiguity of *perichoresis* reappears, because it is very difficult to know whether the speaker is the theologian or the pastor. It would be dangerous to see the result not as *one* fruit of the reflection of Ratzinger the theologian but as *the* exposition of the head of the congregation for the faith.

We only have to think of how different the significance would be if this public dialogue – on the same or other questions of a pope – was not with a philosopher but with a Catholic *theologian*. In fact, this is what is implied in the text quoted from the prologue to his Christology. But the difficulties and even confusion that this type of debate would give rise to is perhaps the best proof of the impossibility of returning to the patristic situation. Cultural differentiation means that what was previously possible in a single *individual* competence must be carried out today amid the difference in the church *communion*.

III   Signs of a resolution

Despite their negative appearance, these observations are meant to help take advantage of both the subjective intention and the objective dynamics that are transforming the situation. Read from a new perspective, the already existing and expressly proclaimed principles display their intrinsic capacity. *Sapientia christiana* Art. 39.1.1. expressly demands 'due freedom to investigate and teach' for theology. And it refers to *Gaudium et Spes* 59, thereby recognizing that it supports the same principles of freedom and autonomy required by the secular sciences: 'Because it arises directly from the rational and social nature of humanity, culture always needs due freedom to develop and proper autonomy to work in accordance with its own principles. Therefore it has the right to be respected and enjoys a certain inviolability...within the limits of the common good.'[7]

Mentioning the common good as a limit shows that this does not imply relativism or anarchy. We have only to distinguish between civil and ecclesiastical common good for this to apply equally to theology. This even has legal recognition in CIC (*Codex Iuris Canonici* = Code of Canon Law) c. 218: 'Those who devote themselves to the sacred sciences enjoy due freedom to investigate, as well as prudently to give their opinion upon everything in which they are expert, while maintaining due submission to the magisterium of the Church'. This is confirmed, in particular, for example, in the famous speeches that John Paul II (who was, of course sympathetic to the theology of the current pope) made in 1980 to theologians in Cologne and Altötting.[8] And Benedict XVI's insistence on the decisive importance of 'reason'–always remembering the need to 'broaden it' towards the specific area of faith–leads in the same direction.

Nevertheless, here too it is necessary to advance in practice, with a working distinction between the pastoral and the theological. This requires two cautions. First, to avoid focusing the discussion too narrowly on different levels of 'compulsoriness' when facing manifestations of the hierarchical magisterium or on the 'theological classification' of doctrines. Second, to point out that continuing to confuse the two magisteria sets up a 'vertical' relationship of *theological* subordination to *pastoral* authority, breaking the 'horizontal' relationship between the two functions. The fundamental obedience must be by *both* magisteria to the *common* good of the Church.

The obedience of the theologian to the *government* of the pastor and the obedience of the pastor to the *scientific* competence of the theologian must be set within that context. It may sound strange at first to speak of obedience on both sides, because this goes against engrained habits. But it is profoundly ecclesial in the communion of services, as Cardinal Ratzinger himself said: 'The pope is not an absolute monarch, whose will is law, but completely the opposite: he must always seek to renounce his will and call the Church to obedience, but he himself must be the first to obey.'[9]

In fact this should be obvious from a careful distinction of levels and functions. For example, it is instructive to read in this context the *Instruction on the ecclesial vocation of the theologian* (24 March 1990). There are statements which state the fundamental *principle:* there are 'different functions: 'ultimately they have the same goal: to keep the people of God in the truth' (No. 21); and 'although...they are different by nature and have different missions that must not be confused, nevertheless they are two vital functions in the Church which should interpenetrate and enrich each other for the service of the people of God' (No. 40).

But the principle is obscured *in practice*, because then the tone and the warnings are always directed towards the virtually unconditional subordination of theology. There also arises the – sometimes painful – impression that people are writing with the feeling that the eyes of authority are upon them, and that this authority must in no way be displeased, but guarded against any possible demand, discrepancy or control. The final part of the *Instruction,* devoted to the 'problem of dissent', constitutes an implacable and unjust analysis, because it is uniquely focused on the possible negative side of all the motives for critical dialogue: 'philosophical liberalism', public opinion, plurality of languages and cultures, theological pluralism, sociological argument, freedom of conscience, human rights, the functioning of democracy. It becomes deaf even to the *sensus fidei* (No. 35) and drastically devalues the distinction between the *cathedra pastoralis* and *magistralis* (note 27). In fact, even in the section devoted to 'relationships of collaboration' it becomes a set of warnings to theologians.

The authority that comes from God is always attributed to the 'magisterium', never directly and expressly to theologians, and it is only they who are asked to exercise caution, scrutiny, patience and prudence. Fair enough, but for the sake of the Church it would be good to apply these demands to the 'magisterium' as well. As an illustrative exercise, look how fruitful for the Church it would be to read the recommendations to theologians as applying also to the 'magisterium': 'Discern in yourself the origin and motives for your critical attitude and let your vision be purified by faith'; 'without ever forgetting that you are also a member of it, you must respect the people of God and commit yourself to give teaching that does no harm at all to the doctrine of the faith'; ' it must be a very disinterested service to the community of believers'. And also: 'a service which essentially includes impartial and objective discussion, fraternal dialogue, openness and readiness to modify your own opinions'; 'even though the doctrine of the faith is not called into question... you must not present your opinions or hypotheses as if they were cast-iron conclusions'; 'critical discernment is necessary as well as real mastery of the problems'.

Approaching the nub of legitimate theological autonomy, the document states something which, without careful qualifications to distinguish between *doctrinal* definition and theological *discourse,* remains too ambiguous. Among the 'hermeneutical rules' for correct interpretation, the theologian must include 'the principle according to which the teaching of the magisterium–thanks to divine assistance–is worth more than the arguments it employs, which are sometimes derived from a particular theology' (No. 34).

In fact, in his speech to members of the Commission, the Pope is more precise and cautious: 'Theologians need the ministry of pastors of the Church, just as the Magisterium needs theologians to serve wholeheartedly with all the ascesis that this implies'. If we take the final admonition, the text appears to indicate that it is addressed to both sides.

To achieve this balance, which is so urgent, two important steps seem necessary: to overcome the negative aspects of power, and positively to activate new possibilities for the Church.

IV Escaping the traps of power

Power tends objectively to monopolize everything. It is invasive. It even tends to deny this invasion. Just as someone in a rage yells that he is not annoyed, power tends to reject criticism by denying its legitimacy *authoritatively,* and if necessary, prohibiting or punishing it. This happens in all spheres and it would be dishonest to deny that it also occurs in the Church. This is not the Church in truth but it is the temptation to which it often succumbs.

The relations between theology and the magisterium are not free from this. The 'linguistic contraction'[10] implied in the restriction of the term 'magisterium' to the *cathedra pastoralis* points to the most serous problem: the (excessive) absorption of the theological charisma by the pastoral ministry. This tends to translate spontaneously into thinking that the hierarchy *alone* is responsible for the faith. As if theologians – although they have a different role – were not equally concerned and responsible for a faith to which they dedicate their energy and their lives.

History saw a great increase of power in the Church, particularly papal power. After the political losses of the nineteenth century, this power attained alarming heights in the religious sphere[11] and in the twentieth century this could even be described as a 'totalitarian claim'.[12] Its dynamic spread tentacles and deployed means that practically conditioned the whole life of the Church.[13] We need only recall a few names – from Chenu to Rahner, von Balthasar and Schillebeeckx, de Lubac to Congar and Bernhard Häring, to name only those now dead – to see its effect on theology, up till today. We hear with good reason of the 'silence, including the silencing of theologians'. If Newman said that without the laity 'the Church would look rather foolish',[14] think of the anomaly of a situation in which theology is gagged.

Indeed, one of the most serious results has been the 'demonization of theological criticism'. Instead of seeing it as a *service,* which from the prophets onwards to Jesus himself has always constituted an indispensable safeguard for the Spirit, it was repeatedly considered to be subversive and destructive. Obviously, as well as the 'pastoral', the 'teaching' cathedra can make mistakes and these need to be corrected. But 'abuse does not take away the use' and it should never be denied that authentic criticism rather than servile, toadying submission represents the only form of true love for the common good.

Let us repeat: Only careful distinction of levels can free the functions to do their proper work. The lack of it introduces confusion. This appears clearly in the problem of propositions which are not declared to be infallible but 'definitive truths', that are not susceptible to discussion.

Without going into detail,[15] I believe that here we have a 'hybrid concept', in which 'pastoral' authority is not confined to regulating the possible *use* of the 'theological' exercise, but enters into the *legality* of its internal functioning. An example may be useful here: in the case of a delicate question that has not yet been sufficiently clarified, it might be legitimate *as a measure of pastoral government* to prohibit its discussion *for a certain period* in the public sphere of the Church. But as a *theological declaration* it would fall epistemologically into the fallacy of deciding *by authority* (with threats and even punishments) about a truth *content*. In questions where publicly serious and responsible theological reasons show that there exists no secure connection with revelation, deciding by authority creates a situation that is unsatisfactory for the Church and theologically illegitimate. With his liberal realism, St Thomas warned: 'If a teacher resolves a question simply through authorities (*nudis auctoritatibus*), the listener will be certain that this is the case but will not advance at all in knowledge or understanding and will proceed empty-handed.'[16]

V Recovering the original experience: fraternal collaboration in common service

Theoretical reflection that insists on its distinct role and on non-interference in it might suggest a self-interested struggle or power conflict. Nothing could be more mistaken. Keeping the distinction must serve only to unite: to unite in radical fellowship in a spirit of *service* and faithful to the *original experience*.

To achieve this, the Council's ecclesiology is vital for its insistence on the *sacramental character* of the *whole* Church, whose essence consists in making the transcendent presence of God the creator–saviour visible and historically effective. The different roles *actualize* this presence, not when such roles are derived from or subject to others, but called to *connect* with the others in the life of the Church as a body. Every function or role is a gift of the Spirit and an empowerment to prolong the gospel mission: 'the whole Church as "salt of the Earth" and "light of the world" (cf. Matt. 5:13f) must bear witness to the truth of Christ that makes us free' (*On the ecclesial mission of the theologian,* No. 3).

Regarding the sacraments in isolation from this fundamental sacramentality has led to their being thought of as a kind of invisible 'miracle', which brings grace as a vertical gift 'from above' without the mediation of the Church.[17] This has had two important effects. First, the consecration meant that attention was paid only to the *specific* sacramentality of the hierarchical function, while disregarding the radical sacramentality that is common to all. Second, this led to that hierarchical function being thought of as *above* the Church and not *within* it or *mediated* by it. Hence, its tendency to absorb the other functions and charismata, which it governs in a legally unconditional way, to the point where we get 'the first seat is judged by nobody'.[18]

Taken literally, this development goes against fundamental teaching, since, even in infallible definitions, the Pope and the Council itself can *only* proclaim what is *in* the Church, which it must gather through consultations with bishops, theologians and the 'sense of the faithful'.[19] Hence, the importance of *reception* and the fundamental priority of the Church's *infallibilitas in credendo*, 'through the sense of the faith' of all the people, when "from bishops to the last of the laity" it manifests its universal agreement' (*Lumen Gentium* 12). That statement is rightly considered to be 'the most innovative ecclesiological novelty of the Second Vatican Council on the magisterium'.[20]

Advancing from Vatican I, Vatican II drew the consequences for the sacramentality of *bishops*. Thus it laid the foundations for the task in hand. That is to stop the post-conciliar tendency to weaken or annul the putting into practice of what has been declared in principle (undermining bishops' conferences and synods by the arrogant claims of the Curia...). And, on the positive side it developed the due, specific sacramentality of all ecclesial functions.

Vatican II also developed the consequences *today* for the relations between the two 'cathedras'. To return to the previous example, look how significant it would be to apply – duly adapted – to the 'teaching cathedra' what the document said for the 'pastoral cathedra': that is, to apply to theologians the statement that 'in virtue of their own charisma they are also bound to share in the building up of the Body of Christ'; they are 'authentic interpreters of the Word of God, whether written or handed down'; 'they receive from the Lord...the mission to teach all people and preach the Gospel to every creature'; their function 'is not something extrinsic to Christian truth or superimposed upon the faith'; they have 'the task of expounding faithfully the deposit of divine revelation'; for them 'there is also divine assistance'; they 'reject the objections and deformations of the faith, and also propose new insights, explanations and applications, with the authority received from Jesus Christ'...

When we have got over our initial surprise, we can see the authentically ecclesial truth of this application. Both cathedras have their proper function, and, inspired by the Spirit, they have a specific role in the life of the Church. Not in vertical subordination but in horizontal collaboration, respecting their intrinsic legal status: one 'commanding and deciding' the other 'investigating and teaching'. The theologian would fail in his mission either by interfering directly in questions of government or by becoming a mere yes-man justifying the pastor's decisions. The pastor would fail in his mission either by allowing himself to be ruled by theologians or by interfering by means of authority in the theologian's specific rationality.

The real difficulty – which perhaps can never completely be resolved – often lies in defining the proper sphere of action for each of them. But it is important to be precise about the right way to go. In fact, by distinguishing between *representation* and *affirmation*, between the conceptual-representative aspect and the judicial–affirmative one, the *Nouvelle Théologie* opened up something fundamental: H. Bouillard showed how, with respect to the 'affirmation' of grace, the big difference between the traditional 'representation' and the 'Aristotelian version of St Thomas did not destroy their true continuity';[21] Rahner's insistence on the character of doctrinal 'regulation of language' points the same way. Today it is not so difficult to see that *faith* in the living presence of Christ in the Eucharist – correctly insisted upon by the pastoral magisterium – can be professed and experienced through the *concepts* of '*transubstantiation*', '*transignificaction*' or '*transfinalization*' and that this updating is right and necessary work by the theological magisterium; or that the *confession* that Jesus in person is alive and glorified can be maintained both by those who *theologically* deny the meaning and possibility of physical apparitions or the 'empty tomb' – considering these to be covert positivism–and by those with the opposite opinion.[22]

Tasks are to be shared out. It is logical that for strictly *theological* problems, the competence belongs to the theologian, because he dedicates to difficult study and explanations the time and effort that the pastor has to use for governing and proclaiming. That is shown by the useful example given by Peter C. Phan in this issue of *Concilium*. This, by the way, is in contrast to the recent example of a theologian friend whose bishop 'examined' him, *Catechism* in hand. Theological conflicts need to be dealt with in fraternal dialogue between equals about *theological reasons;* perhaps in discussions or collaborative monographs, not by decrees or legal processes. Judgment by tribunal would only make sense in those cases which are justified by the negative *results* of fraternal open and competent dialogue. And when the gravity of the case required official intervention, it would be important that all the participants should declare under oath that they have studied the question sufficiently *and* are prepared to seek 'the whole truth and nothing but the truth' (something similar is required in civil courts for much less serious questions).

The need for change is obvious from a history full of mistaken condemnations, resulting from an authoritarian process without any real theological discussion or clarity of procedure. Rahner could write in 1971: 'Today practically all the decisions by Rome between 1900 and 1950 in the field of exegesis and biblical theology...have become antiquated.'[23] And sadly, it is well-known that there are many examples of this.[24]

It may sound harsh to bring this up. But we need to remind ourselves of it because the memory can free the future. Fortunately, we are in a position to do so, because now the ecclesiological foundations can clearly recover the living dynamism of the original experience.

Paul is a good example. Though it can still surprise us and has never been put into practice, his proclamation against any radical inequality between persons still stands as a basic principle today: neither race, nor religious allegiance, nor social inequality, nor difference of gender have any validity in the new being-in-Christ (Gal. 3.28). And above all, there is his heart-warming principle that, in the fellowship of the body that is the Church, there cannot be discrimination for reasons of honour, prestige or power. On the contrary: 'God has so arranged the body, giving greater honour to the inferior member, that there may be no dissension within the body, but the members may have the same care for one another' (1 Cor. 12.24).

Above all, there is still the living example of Jesus, with his energetically expressed appeal to avoid the snares of power, which he indeed suffered in his own flesh. Nothing is more radically opposed to the domination and oppression of the 'rulers of the nations' than his radical principle of service for love's sake, and his insistence that the last should come first: 'It will not be so among you; but whoever wishes to be great among you must be your servant'.

The individual *perichoresis* of the patristic era was frequently admirable but also inevitably limited; now cultural differentiation has made it impossible. Its place must be taken by a communal fulfilment in the living body of the Church, in fraternal collaboration between the different charismata and functions for the common good in the grace of the one Spirit.

Translated by Dinah Livingstone

Notes

1. Cf. Various authors, *Asamblea conjunta obispos–sacerdotes*, Madrid, 1971.
2. M. Iraburu, *Luis Francisco Ladaria y el pecado original*: http://es.catholic.net/sectasapologeticayconversos/745/2347/articulo.php?id=22808.
3. J.M. Iraburu, *Olegario González de Cardedal y la Cristología*: http://es.catholic.net/sectasapologeticayconversos/745/2347/articulo.php?id=22809. Incidentally, this writer criticizes González with similar arguments to those he uses to criticize my theology in a misleading exposition with false attributions (together with the theology of C. Theobald y J. Moingt): cf. A. Torres Queiruga, 'Aclaración sobre mi teología. Respuesta a un diagnóstico de Olegario González de Cardedal', *Iglesia Viva* 235 (2008), pp. 103–14 (which also reproduces his text).
4. 'Kirchliches Lehramt und theologische Wissenschaft', in *id., Die schiefen Wände des Lehrhauses*, Freiburg im Breisgau, 1988, pp. 105–35; reproduced with other works in: *id., Teologia, Scienza, Chiesa. Saggi di teologia fondamentale*, 1988, pp. 237–79 (I shall quote from this edition).
5. Cf. M. Seckler, *op. cit.*, pp. 250–3.
6. Y. Congar, 'Pour une histoire sémantique du terme magisterium', *RScPhTh* (*Revue des sciences philosophiques et théologiques* = *Review of Philosophical and Theological Sciences* 60 (1976), pp. 85–97; *id.*, 'Bref historique des formes du 'magistère' et de ses relations avec les docteurs', *RScPhTh* 60 (1976), pp. 99–112; E. Vilanova, 'El ejercicio del poder doctrinal en los siglos XII y XIII', in: various authors, *Teología y Magisterio*, Salamanca, 1987, pp. 115–38.
7. A brief summary can be seen in H. Schwendenwein, 'Lehramt, akademisches' in: ³*LThK* (*Lexikon für Theologie und Kirche*) 3, pp. 750–1 and A. Hollerbach, 'Freiheit der Wissenschaft in der Kirche': ³*LThK* 4, pp. 113–5.
8. See the almost enthusiastic assessment by M. Seckler, *op. cit.*, pp. 260–3.
9. *Convocados en el camino de la fe*, Madrid, 2004, pp. 223–48. 240f (I take the reference from S. Pié-Ninot, *Eclesiología*, Salamanca 2007, p. 489).
10. M. Seckler, *op. cit.*, p. 194.
11. J. M. Castillo, 'La exaltación del poder magisterial en el siglo XIX', in: various authors, *Teología y Magisterio*, Salamanca, 1987, pp. 139–60.

12. M. Seckler, *op. cit.*, pp. 257–9.
13. See the dispassionate but crude analysis by J. M. Mardones, 'El Magisterio como poder', in: various authors, *Teología y Magisterio*, pp. 161–184.
14. 'Well, without them, the Church would look rather foolish', quoted by P. Prini, *El cisma soterrado*, Valencia, 2003, p. 107; cf. also M. Trevor, *John H. Newman*, Salamanca, 1989, p. 205.
15. Of special interest is the discussion between L. Örsy, 'Von der Autorität kirchlichen Dokumente. Eine Fallstudie zum Apostolischen Schreiben "Ad tuendam fidem"', *Stimmen der Zeit* 216 (1998), pp. 735–40; 'Antwort an Kardinal Ratzinger', *Stimmen der Zeit* 217 (1999), pp. 305–16; J. Ratzinger, 'Stellungnahme', *Stimmen der Zeit* 217 (1999), pp. 169–71.
16. *Quodlibet IV*,q. 9,a. 3. Cf. also P. Valadier, *La condición cristiana*, Santander, 2005, pp. 25–257.
17. On this delicate and important question cf. A. Torres Queiruga, 'Los sacramentos hoy. Acontecimiento real sin intervencionismo divino', in: É. Gaziaux (ed.), *Philosophie et Théologie*, Louvain, 2007, pp. 485–508.
18. S. Vacca, *Prima sedes a nemine iudicatur*, Rome, 1993.
19. Cf., with special reference to Newman, J. Coulson, 'The Magisterium of the Church &c', *Concilium* 108 (1975), pp. 253–64.
20. S. Pié-Nitot, p. 495; cf. pp. 495–9; the whole of Part II is worth consulting for its balance and information, pp. 213–607.
21. *Conversion et grâce chez S. Thomas d'Aquin*, Paris, 1944; mainly the conclusion, pp. 219–20.
22. Incidentally, this is a good example of the need for caution, when it is claimed that *empirical* apparitions are a necessary basis to *faith* in the Resurrection. In his speech made on the occasion of the Ratzinger Prize, the Pope issued a timely warning in his comment on the temptation in the desert: 'But it is not enough for them, so they want to put God "to the test". They want to submit him to experiment. He is, so to speak, interrogated and submitted to a procedure of *experimental proof* [my italics]. This way of using reason has reached its peak development during the modern period, within the natural sciences. Today experimental reason broadly presents itself as the sole form of rationality declared to be scientific'. I stressed the unconscious but very influential 'empiricism' in this question in *Repensar la resurrección*, Madrid, 2003, pp. 96–103.
23. 'Libertad de la teología y ortodoxia eclesial' *Concilium* 66, 1971, pp. 410–27, on p. 415.
24. Cf. J. I. González-Faus, *La autoridad de la verdad*, Santander, 2006, and the 'Forum' in this issue of *Concilium*.

N.B. This article was submitted to Concilium in December 2011, before the publication of the new CTI document (8 March 2012) on the prospects, principles and criteria of theology todady. I could not take this significantly more cautious and balanced result into account.

Theologians and Bishops: Good Procedures Promote Collaboration

JAMES A. CORIDEN

I A shocking intervention

The action taken against Elizabeth Johnson by the United States Conference of Catholic Bishops Committee on Doctrine[1] shocked the North American Catholic theological world for three distinct reasons. The first was the high esteem in which Johnson is held as a theologian, and the widespread acceptance of and praise for her book *Quest for the Living God: Mapping Frontiers in the Theology of God*,[2] the work targeted by the Bishops' Committee. The second was the secretive procedure employed by the Committee that neither gave advance notice to Johnson of the investigation nor offered her any opportunity to explain or defend her book until after their statement was made public. This despite the existence of the Conference's own procedural document *Doctrinal Responsibilities: Approaches to Promoting Cooperation and Resolving Misunderstandings between Bishops and Theologians*.[3] These suggested procedures called for both advance notice to the theologian and ample opportunities for explanation, dialogue, and self-defence. The third reason was the misinterpretations and distortions in the Committee's own statement of evaluation of Johnson's book. Johnson said that her book, as a work of theology, was thoroughly misunderstood and consistently misrepresented in the Committee's statement.[4]

The shock waves resonated in a statement of response from the Board of Directors of the Catholic Theological Society of America and in a resolution approved by the members of the CTSA at their convention in June 2011.[5] The CTSA Board raised three points of concern: 1) that the bishops did not follow the procedures set forth in their own document *Doctrinal Responsibilities*; 2) the misreading of Professor Johnson's work in the statement; and 3) the troubling implications that the statement presented for the exercise of their vocation as theologians. The resolution of the CTSA membership focused on the bishops' failure to use the procedures suggested by *Doctrinal Responsibilities,* and it recommended that the Conference of Bishops should establish a committee to evaluate the procedures of the Committee on Doctrine that led to their statement on Johnson's book.

The officers and board of directors of the College Theology Society, which is made up largely of those theologians who teach at the undergraduate level, endorsed the statement of the CTSA board and went on to praise Johnson's book as exemplifying a compelling style of Catholic theology that engages many different kinds of undergraduate students. 'Her theology is credited with plumbing the depths of the received Catholic tradition as found in the diverse scriptural and historical witnesses of faith while investigating pressing issues and searching for ever deeper understanding.'[6]

A welter of issues lie imbedded in this controversial intervention of the American bishops' doctrinal committee, theological issues such as the attributes of God, human language about the reality of God, and the nature of the Trinity, and political issues such as the composition of the committee (whose members are chosen by its chair), and the orientation of its staff and non-bishop consultants, some of whom are openly aligned with the right wing of Catholic theologians. Another, more basic issue, still not adequately aired or agreed upon, is that of the interdependent roles of bishops, theologians, and faithful in the Church's teaching function (the *munus docendi*).[7]

However, underlying these sometimes divisive issues, they share an ecclesial common ground.

II Ecclesial communion is our common context

We are all in this together: theologians, bishops, and baptized believers. This is our theological conviction,[8] but it also finds strong canonical expression. The Church's canons remind us that we are all members of the Christian faithful, sharers in Christ's own prophetic function, and that we are all called to exercise the Church's mission, including its teaching mission, in the world (c. 204).[9] We are linked to Christ by the ties of profession of faith, the sacraments, and governance, and thus fully in communion with one another in the Church (c. 205). In other words, we are all on the same team, engaged in a common enterprise, not on opposing sides.

More specifically, in regard to the Church's teaching function, the canons insist that Christ has entrusted the deposit of faith to all of us in the Church, so that, with the assistance of the Holy Spirit, we might protect revealed truth reverently, examine it closely, proclaim it faithfully, and preach the Gospel to all peoples (c. 747). Each one of us is bound to seek the truth in matters related to God and the Church, and each one has the duty and right to embrace and observe the truth discovered (c. 748). We are all witnesses of the gospel message by word and the example of a Christian life, in virtue of our baptism and confirmation (c. 759). We are not strangers or adversaries, but members of the same body, closely related, of common faith and common cause, obliged to show love for one another.[10]

This shared commitment within our ecclesial context calls for mutual respect, dialogue, and cooperation between bishops, theologians, and other members of the Christian faithful. A central theme of this entire topic emphasizes the importance of a climate of cooperation, of conversation, and collaboration within which misunderstandings or conflicts can be successfully resolved. It is the assistance of the Holy Spirit that leads the Church forward on its way of God's truth. This growth in understanding comes about through contemplation, study, and spiritual experience.[11] The guidance of the Holy Spirit cannot be readily discerned amidst the adversarial din of duelling press releases.

III Focus on procedures: an example from the past

In this essay I shall focus my attention on the procedural issues rather than the theological debates. How do writings come to the attention of doctrinal committees of episcopal conferences, how are they investigated, when are the authors involved, who makes the theological judgment on the publications, and how is that judgment expressed?

A truly remarkable example of positive collaboration between bishops and theologians was the development of the National Conference of Catholic Bishops' (NCCB, now the US Conference of Catholic Bishops [USCCB]) document entitled *Doctrinal Responsibilities,* referred to above.

The document that was approved and issued by the NCCB in 1989 derived from an initiative taken by the Catholic Theological Society of America (CTSA) in 1980, a collaborative effort of the CTSA and the Canon Law Society of America (CLSA) in 1982, and further collaboration between the two societies, individual bishops, and the doctrinal committee of the NCCB. It is helpful to recall how this extraordinary joint effort came about.

In 1979, widespread concern among theologians over the recent interventions of the Congregation for the Doctrine of the Faith (CDF) related to the Christological writings of Edward Schillebeeckx and regarding the book *Human Sexuality: New Directions in American Catholic Thought*[12] caused the CTSA president, William Hill, OP, to name a committee to search 'for more cooperative and constructive relations between theologians and the Church's teaching authority.'[13] The committee's report described the state of the question and proposed a joint committee with the CLSA to develop a 'set of norms to guide the resolution of difficulties which may arise in the relationship between theologians and the magisterium in North America'.[14]

The joint committee, chaired by Leo O'Donovan, SJ, and consisting of three other theologians and three canonists,[15] was appointed in September, 1980. The members wrote six background papers on the rights and responsibilities of bishops and theologians, and evaluations of the procedures available to settle misunderstandings or conflicts between them. The committee added a consensus statement, 'In Service to the Gospel', that summarized their findings and recommendations.

This 'Report of the Joint Committee', entitled *Cooperation Between Theologians and the Ecclesiastical Magisterium*, was published in 1982.[16] The committee continued its work, entering into further collaboration with bishops, theologians, and canonists, and formulated the procedural document, *Doctrinal Responsibilities*. This work product was presented to and approved unanimously by the national meetings of both societies (CTSA and CLSA) in 1983.[17] The document was then submitted to the NCCB Committee on Doctrine, where it was revised, amended, and sent out for consultation with the full body of bishops in 1988. It was subject to a consultation at the Holy See,[18] and was then approved overwhelmingly (the vote was 214 to 9) by the body of American bishops in June, 1989.[19] The development and approval of *Doctrinal Responsibilities* represent an exemplary achievement in ecclesial collaboration.

IV   The content of Doctrinal Responsibilities

Doctrinal Responsibilities is divided into three sections. The first, 'The Context of Ecclesial Responsibilities', sketches the active participation that all members of the Body of Christ have in the proclamation of the Gospel, and then the particular rights and responsibilities of bishops and of theologians. The second section, 'Promoting Cooperation and Informal

Dialogue', speaks of the climate of ongoing cooperation between bishops and theologians, and how that will help them to grow in respect and trust for one another. It then recommends various specific ways in which bishops and theologians can implement structured cooperation in their common service to the Gospel.

Their cooperation will aid their doctrinal dialogue because they will come to know one another as faithful persons with distinct but inseparable services to perform in the one Church.

The third section is entitled, 'A Possibility for Formal Doctrinal Dialogue.' It sets out in detail a suggested procedure to deal with doctrinal disputes between bishops and theologians in dioceses. It is intended to be flexible and adaptable to local situations and needs. The document makes clear that its suggested procedures are not church law, but guidelines that may be followed when needed. The dialogue is for purposes of mutual understanding, to determine the facts and their theological and pastoral implications. The dialogue is prior to any consideration of any judicial or administrative action. 'Briefly stated, the purpose of formal doctrinal dialogue is to determine the nature and gravity of the issue at dispute as well as its pastoral significance and to achieve an agreement between the parties.'[20]

The procedures are reasonable and laid out in a series of carefully described tasks. (They may have been too detailed; they may have appeared complex and daunting to some who considered using them.) But the document concludes with this conviction: 'We believe that, with the guidance of the Spirit, the many different parts of the body of Christ can be knit together in justice and love, and thereby become more truly themselves before God. In seeking clear and equitable ways to resolve disagreements about our faith, we recommit ourselves to being a Church that is one and open, a genuine community of grace sharing the truth freely given to it'.[21]

It is only fair to note that the second and third sections of *Doctrinal Responsibilities* were intended primarily for application to individual bishops and theologians within their dioceses; they were not explicitly directed to the Committee on Doctrine of the Bishops' Conference.[22] However, the document did not limit its application to individuals, and envisioned its use in any doctrinal conflicts that might occur between theologians and bishops, not excluding those bishops on the Committee on Doctrine. The formal authority of the document as well as its intrinsic qualities – judicious, even-handed, reverent, open, and fair – argue for its use by the conference committee, at least to the adoption of its procedures by analogy.[23]

The process set forth in *Doctrinal Responsibilities* was recommended more recently by the Bisholps' Conference for use in the NCCB 'Guidelines Concerning the Academic *Mandatum* in Catholic Universities (Canon 812).'[24] Canon 812 of the 1983 *Code of Canon Law* stated that 'It is necessary that those who teach theological disciplines in any institute of higher studies have a mandate (*mandatum*) from the competent ecclesiastical authority.' This canonical regulation was strenuously resisted during the *Code* revision process and was not enforced in the United States for many years after the *Code* was promulgated. Most bishops, theologians, and college administrators saw no need for it. Pope John Paul II's 1990 apostolic constitution on Catholic higher education (*Ex corde Ecclesiae*) again called for the *mandatum* to be sought and granted. The US Conference of Bishops again resisted making it a requirement. Their negotiations with the Congregation for Catholic Education over the application of norms of *Ex corde* went on for ten years.

An 'application' was finally approved by the Congregation on 3 May 2001, and on 15 June 2001, the membership of the Conference accepted a set of 'guidelines' for a process of requesting and granting (or withdrawing) the *mandatum*. It was in this context that the processes of *Doctrinal Responsibilities* were recommended. When a bishop contemplates withholding or withdrawing the *mandatum*, the 'doctrinal dialogue' process should be employed.[25]

The point here is that the procedures for dealing with doctrinal differences approved overwhelmingly by the Conference of Bishops in 1989 and recommended again for use in 2001, were not used or even alluded to in the intervention of the Committee on Doctrine against Elizabeth Johnson's book in 2011.

Doctrinal Responsibilities has not been replaced, remanded, or revoked. It is not well-known, but it should prove to be of service. The document's official endorsement by the Bishops' Conference, that is, by the entire body of bishops and not only by a committee of the Conference, gives it an enhanced status. Its renewed recommendation by the Conference 22 years later, in 2001, further enhanced its authority, which makes its neglect by the Committee on Doctrine in 2011 even more inexcusable.

At the time of the Committee's action on Johnson's book in March of

2011, the Committee had no published guidelines or procedures. This was soon to change.

V   Committee on Doctrine Protocol (2011)

A few months after the Committee's statement regarding Elizabeth Johnson's book, the Committee adopted an internal 'protocol' to guide the Committee in responding to requests for its assistance. The brief document (five double-spaced pages) is designated as a 'draft' for the Committee's present use, and dated 19 August.[26] The requests for the Committee's assistance might come from a bishop, another USCCB committee, or from a proposal for Committee action by one of its own members. (There is no mention of requests from the CDF.)

The protocol outlines three stages of response:

1) *Preliminary Analysis*: The Executive Director prepares a report for the chair of the Committee giving the origin of the request for assistance, the nature of the doctrinal issues in question, the genre and intended audience of the writing or statement, its dissemination and pastoral implications, and published reviews of the publication. The chair reports the results of this preliminary analysis to the Committee at its next meeting.

2) *Scholarly Review*: The Committee may determine that a more thorough evaluation of the writing is warranted, and 'ideally' that task is assigned to 'two or more experts' by the Executive Director in consultation with the Committee chair. Their evaluations should address the positive aspects of the writing, areas of legitimate differences of opinion, and instances where the writing departs from the Church's teaching on faith and morals. The *Catechism of the Catholic Church* provides a reliable guide for the evaluations. The evaluations are submitted to the Committee for deliberation.

3) *Options for Response*: The Committee may determine that no further action is needed.

If, however, the Committee determines that some action is warranted, one or more of the following options may form a suitable response:

(a) The Committee may offer its evaluation to the proper diocesan bishop or refer the bishop to a theologian who may be contacted directly. 'The task of monitoring and evaluating theological works belongs properly to the diocesan bishop.'

(b) The Committee may refer the matter to the Congregation for the

Doctrine of the Faith, due to the gravity of the teachings in question or their impact outside the country.

(c) The Committee may refer the matter to another USCCB committee.

(d) The Committee itself may take action in one or more ways:

1. Engage the author in a constructive dialogue resulting in the publication of required clarifications or corrections. 2. Encourage a scholar or group of scholars to publish a critique of the writing in their own name. 3. Disseminate a published scholarly review of the writing. 4. Authorize for publication a critique of the writing in the name of the Executive Director (with prior approval of the USCCB General Secretary) or of a consultant to the Committee. 5. Designate the Committee chair to publish a critique of the writing in his own name (with the prior approval of the USCCB President). 6. Issue a statement in its own name (an extraordinary action requiring the authorization of the Administrative Committee).

Before the submission of the Committee's statement to the Administrative Committee the author of the writing 'may be invited to respond to the Committee's observations in writing.' The Committee reserves the right to publish its statements without prior consultation with the author 'if it judges that intervention is needed for the pastoral guidance of the Catholic faithful.'

The author's ordinary or competent major superior should be duly notified of actions being undertaken by the Committee. The Committee's actions ought always to be conducted with a respect for the natural right to a good reputation and to the lawful freedom of inquiry (*Code of Canon Law*, cc. 218, 220).

VI Comment on the new protocol

Some publicly-known procedure is better than none at all. At very least, bishops, theologians, and the Catholic faithful are now aware of the present investigative process of the Committee on Doctrine.

The protocol appears to be a scaled-down version of the 'Regulations for Doctrinal Examination' of the CDF (1997); it follows a parallel path. Its aim is to determine the conformity of the published writings of individuals or groups to the Church's authentic teaching on faith or morals. The reliable guide for this evaluation is stated to be the *Catechism of the Catholic Church*.

The procedures are initiated and progress to their third stage without notice to the author under investigation, or to his or her bishop or religious superior. If the Committee, at its action stage, chooses to engage the author in a dialogue, the stated result will be that the author will publish requisite clarifications or corrections. In other words, at this stage there is an assumption that the author is either ambiguous, in error, or both.

By contrast, the purpose of the 'formal doctrinal dialogue' proposed in *Doctrinal Responsibilities* is 'to determine the facts and their theological and pastoral implications, and thereby to resolve any misunderstandings between bishops and theologians.' It is to explore the nature and gravity of the issue at dispute as well as its pastoral significance and to achieve an agreement between the parties. The process is dialogal from the outset, there is no secrecy, and the level of confidentiality of the proceedings is a matter of agreement between the parties. There is an explicit presupposition of sound doctrine, which holds unless it is refuted by contrary evidence.[27]

VII   Focus on procedures: still a need at present

The successful initiative taken thirty years ago that resulted in *Doctrinal Responsibilities*, needs to be revisited. A joint committee of the Catholic Theological Society of America and the Canon Law Society of America (plus the College Theology Society) should undertake three specific projects:

1. study the 'Regulations for Doctrinal Examination', of the CDF and make recommendations for their improvement.[28] More up-to-date and fairer procedures would enhance the Congregation's own function as well as afford greater justice to theologians. 2. re-examine *Doctrinal Responsibilities*, and suggest modifications to make its procedures for doctrinal dialogue and dispute resolution simpler and more expeditious. 3. study the role of the USCCB Committee on Doctrine and suggest more appropriate procedures for its investigations and assistance to bishops;[29] models exist in the 2001 NCCB guidelines related to the *mandatum*, in the processes recommended in *Doctrinal Responsibilities*, and in the statements of other episcopal conferences.[30]

In conclusion

'Both bishops and theologians are engaged in a necessary though complementary service to the church that requires ongoing and mutually respectful dialogue.' So said the American bishops in 2001.[31] In keeping with that statement, does it not seem more appropriate, when there are complaints about some theologian's writing, or there is a request for the assistance of the Committee on Doctrine regarding the same, to hew to the path of dialogue and discussion rather than the path of confidential inquiry and surprise public statement? Dialogue was the method recommended by the International Theological Commission (ITC) in 1976,[32] and the method approved overwhelmingly by the American bishops' conference in 1989 and again in 2001. Why was it abandoned in 2011?

As the joint CTSA/CLSA committee concluded in 1982, 'In seeking clear and equitable ways to address disagreements that arise about our faith, we can recommit ourselves to being a Church that is one and open, a genuine community of grace which exists to share the truth that has been freely given to it.'[33]

Notes

1. 'Statement on *Quest for the Living God: Mapping the Frontiers in the Theology of God*, by Sister Elizabeth A. Johnson', 24 March 2011. *Origins* 40:43 (April 7, 2011), pp. 704–11.
2. New York, 2007.
3. Washington, USCC, 1989.
4. The defects in the Committee's analysis were detailed by Johnson in 'To Speak Rightly of the Living God', 38 pages of 'observations' sent to the Committee on Doctrine on 1 June 2011. *Origins* 41:9 (7 July 2011), pp. 29–47. On 11 October 2011, the Committee on Doctrine issued an eleven-page 'Response to Observations', that basically reaffirmed its original criticisms and concluded by stating 'the Committee on Doctrine believes that it is its duty to state publicly that on several critical points the book is seriously inadequate as a presentation of the Catholic understanding of God.' 'Response to Sister Elizabeth Johnson', *Origins* 41:22 (3 November 2011), pp. 350–5, at p. 355.
5. The resolution, which passed on 10 June, in San Jose, CA, by a vote of 147 to 1, with 2 abstentions, is recorded in *National Catholic Reporter*, issue of 11 June 2011.
6. *National Catholic Reporter*: http://ncronline.org/print/24158 accessed 19 April 2011.
7. These nuanced relationships were well described in the NCCB document *Doctrinal Responsibilities*, 'The Context of Ecclesial Responsibilities', pp. 3–10.
8. *Lumen gentium* 12, 31.
9. Canons are paraphrased from the 1983 *Code of Canon Law*, Latin–English Edition, Canon Law Society of America, Washington, DC, 1999.
10. *Doctrinal Responsibilities* opens with a well-balanced statement of what bishops and theologians have in common, 'Context and Principles', pp. 3–4.
11. Affirmed in *Lumen Gentium 1,* and *Dei verbum 8.*
12. New York, 1977. This book was a product of a CTSA committee and edited by its chair, Anthony Kosnik. It was the subject of a 1977 statement of the NCCB Committee on Doctrine dated 15 November 1977. 'Bishops' Doctrinal Committee Responds to Book on Sexuality', *Origins* 7:24 (1 December 1977), pp. 376–8. The CDF notification, 'Doctrinal Congregation Criticises "Human Sexuality" Book', is found in *Origins* 9:11 (30 August 1979), pp. 167–9.

13. 'CTSA Committee Report on Cooperation between Theologians and the Church's Teaching Authority', *CTSA Proceedings* 35 (1980), p. 325.
14. *Ibid.*, p. 331.
15. John Boyle, Patrick Granfield, OSB, Jon Nilson; John Alesandro, Robert Carlson, James Provost.
16. Edited by Leo O'Donovan, it was issued as a 189-page booklet by the Canon Law Society of America.
17. The document as presented to the two societies is found on pp. 261–84 of the *CLSA Proceedings* 45 (1983). The CLSA minutes report the unanimous votes of both societies on pp. 328–9.
18. The concerns of the CDF are reflected in a communication from Archbishop Bovone, the secretary of the congregation, 'Development of Text Regarding Relationship between Bishops and Theologians' (11 November 1988) *Canon Law Digest* 12, pp. 476–8; also in *Origins* 18 (1988), pp. 389–91.
19. The full title of the document is *Doctrinal Responsibilities: Approaches to Promoting Cooperation and Resolving Misunderstandings between Bishops and Theologians*. It was published by the USCC in 1989 as a 29-page booklet (publication number 284–5). This sustained collaboration between the Bishops' Conference and the two professional societies is detailed in *Doctrinal Responsibilities*, p. 1 and footnote 1.
20. *Doctrinal Responsibilities*, p. 15.
21. *Ibid.*, p. 24.
22. *Ibid.*, pp. 1, 4. Archbishop Dolan, President of the Conference, made this point in his letter to John Thiel, President of the CTSA on 7 July 2011
23. This view was eloquently articulated by Michael Buckley, '"Doctrinal Responsibilities"': evenhanded, open and fair', *National Catholic Reporter* (14 October 2011), pp. 17, 22.
24. Dated 15 June 2001, and published in *Origins* 31:7 (28 June 2001), pp. 128–31.
25. 'Guidelines Concerning the *Mandatum*', *Origins* 31:7 (28 June 2001), p. 130.
26. The text was graciously provided to me by the Executive Director of the Secretariat on Doctrine of the USCCB on 27 October 2011.
27. *Doctrinal Responsibilities*, p. 14.
28. Issued 29 June 1997. Available on the Vatican website; also published in *Doctrine & Life* 47:8 (October 1997), pp. 499–506 (also in *Origins* 27:13 (11 September 1997), pp. 221–4, and in *CLGBI Newsletter* 112 (December 1997), pp. 7–17*)*.
29. Some parameters for the work of doctrinal commissions are articulated in the CDF circular letter of 25 November 1990, and repeated in Adriano Garuti, 'Collaboration between the Congregation for the Doctrine of the Faith and Doctrinal Commissions of Episcopal Conferences', USCC, *Proclaiming the Truth of Jesus Christ: Papers from the Vallombrosa Meeting* (Washington, DC: USCC, 2000), pp. 53–9. Also note the set of 'concrete proposals' on pp. 7–10.
30. For example, the 1972 statement of the Conference of German Bishops, 'The Procedure for Settling Grievances in Matters of Doctrine', and the 1999 statement of the Australian Catholic Conference of Bishops, 'The Examination of Theological Orthodoxy'.
31. 'Guidelines Concerning the *Mandatum*', *Origins* 31:7 (28 June 2001), p. 129.
32. ITC, *Theses on the Relationship between the Ecclesiastical Magisterium and Theology* (Washington, DC: USCC, 1977) Nos 10–2.
33. *Cooperation between Theologians and the Ecclesiastical Magisterium* (Washington, DC: CLSA, 1982), p. 189.

Teaching as Learning: an Asian View

PETER C. PHAN

Allow me to begin with a true story. In 1988, I was asked to give a series of continuing-education lectures to the clergy of a newly-created diocese. On the first evening, the bishop invited me to his office for pre-prandial drinks. As we sat down, he confessed that he had not read a theology book from cover to cover since his ordination to the priesthood. He asked if I would give him a quick overview of the most significant recent theological developments. Truth to tell, I was not shocked that he had not perused theological tomes – I had suspected that bishops were too busy to do serious theological reading. What surprised and humbled me was that a bishop wanted to learn about what was going on in theology, even from a budding theologian. He wanted to be a learner rather than and/or before being a teacher as he began his episcopal ministry.

This story came to my mind as I reflected on 'Theologians, Bishops, and the Magisterium'. Of course the theme can be approached from a variety of perspectives. Given the current adversarial relations between bishops (including the Pope and the Roman Curia, especially the Congregation for the Doctrine of the Faith) and theologians – the latest case being the shameful treatment of Elizabeth Johnson's *Quest for the Living God* by the US bishops' Committee on Doctrine – it is understandable that broaching the subject of relations between bishops and theologians immediately brings up for discussion issues such as freedom of research and publication, the different functions of theology and catechesis, the distinction between the '*magisterium cathedrae pastoralis*' (teaching office of the pastoral chair) of bishops and the '*magisterium cathedrae magisterialis*' (teaching office of the professorial chair) of theologians and their respective competencies, the categories of infallible and authentic teachings, and the legitimacy of 'dissent' in the latter, the canonical procedures designed to guarantee fairness and protect the rights of the accused, and a host of associated theological and canonical problems.

Admittedly, all of these issues are important, and they should not be skirted, especially because of the immense harm that will be inflicted on the Church when theological distinctions are blurred and legal procedures ignored. Fortunately, eminent theologians and canonists have carefully categorized the various exercises of the episcopal magisterium, their respective authorities, and the corresponding kinds of assent due to them, and have proposed effective ways to promote fruitful collaboration and harmonious relation between theologians and bishops. Works by Francis Sullivan, Ladislas Örsy, Thomas Rausch, and Richard Gaillardetz, to cite only a few English-language authors, remain indispensable reference tools for their historical thoroughness, theological depth, and pastoral sensitivity.[1]

I Teaching and Learning

While deeply indebted to these authors' insights, I would like to examine the relations between bishops and theologians by focusing on their roles not as teachers but as *learners* of the faith. My approach goes against the grain of the standard treatment of the episcopal magisterium and the teaching role of theologians and the relations between them. A common practice of this standard treatment is to regard both bishops and theologians primarily as teachers (*magistri*) and then attempt to circumscribe their respective competencies and authorities. It is *de rigueur* to point out that one essential difference between these two kinds of teachers is that the Pope by himself (*ex cathedra*) and all the bishops in communion with the Pope, either in solemn occasion (e. g., in ecumenical councils) or spread throughout the world (the ordinary universal magisterium), can, with specific conditions, teach infallibly, whereas theologians never can. Furthermore, it is taught that the episcopal magisterium, even when it is not infallible, is 'authentic', or more exactly, 'authoritative', that is, 'teachers endowed with the authority of Christ', to whose teaching the faithful must adhere with 'religious docility (*obsequium*) of the will and intellect' (*Lumen Gentium*, No. 25).

Historically, bishops and theologians together have played an indispensable role in the formulation of the official teachings of the Church, especially when the majority of bishops were theologians, as in the patristic period, and this close collaboration between the two teaching bodies persisted even until the Council of Trent (1545–63). However, as bishops functioned increasingly as pastoral administrators and theologians carved out an autonomous niche in the – often secular –academy, their relation has often been strained if not hostile, with a brief respite during the Second Vatican Council (1962–65), when theologians were appointed as *periti*. In recent decades, however, with the disciplining of several theologians by the Congregation for the Doctrine of the Faith and national episcopal conferences, the issue of the relationship between bishops and theologians has become an urgent and fraught topic once again.

In this context, I suggest that the traditional approach of considering bishops and theologians primarily if not exclusively as *teachers*, while valid, is unhelpful. First, despite all the careful and painstaking fence-building to prevent conflicts between the *magisterium cathedrae pastoralis* and the *magisterium cathedrae magisterialis*, a sense of competition and turf war is always looming between these two, albeit unequal, *magisteria*. Second, detaching teaching from learning perpetuates the harmful distinction between the *ecclesia docens* (the teaching Church) and the *ecclesia discens* (the learning Church), obscuring the fact the entire Church is both learning and teaching. Third, this separation promotes the exercise of teaching as a juridical act requiring assent (alternatively, occasioning dissent) rather than fostering a dynamic process of continuous learning within the bishops and theologians themselves and facilitating mutual teaching between them and the rest of the Church.

To alleviate the tension between episcopal magisterium and theologians, I suggest that we view both bishops and theologians primarily as *learners* of the faith. At first sight, this seems to be something so simple and easy as to need no thought, since people cannot teach what they do not know, or, as the Latin adage puts it tersely, *nemo dare potest quod non habet* (you cannot give what you do not have). Yet it is interesting to note that neither Vatican I nor Vatican II, when speaking of the magisterium of the pope and bishops, ever mentioned them as *learners*. Apparently, episcopal ordination is believed to confer not only the power (and duty) to teach but the gift of actual, as it were infused, knowledge, and magically transform the ordinands (including priests) into theological experts, or to put it more modestly, teachers with passable theological competence. Sadly, experience tells us that this Cinderella-type transmogrification does not – and cannot – occur, and pretensions to teaching authority in virtue of ordination appear as a cover-up for ignorance and a grab for power (I used to tell seminarians that the laying-on of episcopal hands does not change an F into an A.)

The questions I intend to raise here do not concern merely pedagogy (e.g., how and what can you teach if you do not know anything?) but are properly theological. What would the theological and ecclesial implications be for our understanding of the teaching function of the faith (*magisterium*) if we were to see bishops and theologians as *learners* of the faith *precisely in their roles as teachers of the faith*? To put it more starkly, what are the doctrinal and ecclesiological consequences of saying that bishops and theologians can be teachers *only in so far as they are learners and must remain so for life*? How will this affect our theology of the teaching ministry (*munus docendi*) of bishops and theologians, what they teach, how they do so, and how they should relate to each other? I shall now try to explore these and other questions, drawing on insights from the Asian understanding of teacher and teaching.

II Jesus as a Learner

Vatican II repeatedly asserts that bishops receive from Christ 'the mission of teaching all peoples' (*Lumen Gentium*, no. 24). That this image of Jesus as teacher is all-pervasive in the New Testament needs no elaboration. Teaching is described as one of Jesus' main activities during his ministry, besides preaching, healing, and exorcizing. 'Teacher (rabbi) is the title his disciples and the crowd regularly use to address him. He is said to teach 'as one having authority' (Matt. 7.29). (We also hear that the Holy Spirit will teach the disciples everything and will remind them of all that Jesus has said to them [John 14.25)].) Therefore the bishops continue the teaching ministry of Jesus and do so 'in the name of Christ', remembering and learning what Jesus has said, under the guidance of the Holy Spirit (*Lumen Gentium*, No. 25).

Unfortunately, this emphasis on Jesus as teacher has glossed over the fact he was also a learner. Admittedly, only indirect references are made to his learning activities. It is said that after his return to Nazareth from his visit to Jerusalem and three-day stay in the temple, the boy Jesus 'was obedient' to his parents and 'increased in wisdom and in years' (Luke 2.52, *NRSV*). Though the Gospels do not tell us anything about Jesus' formal education, it can safely be assumed that he did receive schooling, most probably at the village synagogue, since he knew how to read Hebrew. In addition, he must have learned, as an apprentice, his trade as carpenter (*tektōn*). During his ministry Jesus was 'amazed' at the faith of the centurion (Matt. 8.10) and at the lack of faith of his townsfolk (Mark 6.6), thereby learning something he had not known. More importantly, in the Johannine Gospel, in which Jesus is presented as the Word of God incarnate and the teacher and revealer par excellence, he is reported to have affirmed that all that he taught he had heard and learned from the Father: 'I have told you everything that I have heard from the Father' (John 15.15). In other words, Jesus is the perfect revealer and teacher because and in so far as he is a perfect hearer and learner. His teaching is derived from his learning.

Jesus' dependence on his learning from the Father is rooted in his more fundamental dependence on, and more precisely, his personal union with, the Father. In response to those who challenged his authority, Jesus said: 'I assure you that the Son can do nothing of his own accord, but only what he sees the Father doing. What the Son does is always modelled on what the Father does' (John 5.19). This unity is described in terms of mutual indwelling: 'I am in the Father and the Father is in me' (John 14.10–11). According to the Letter to the Hebrews, 'Son though he was, he had to prove the meaning of obedience through all that he suffered' (5.8). Thus, Jesus could teach 'as one having authority' because he was an obedient learner from the Father and, significantly, through his suffering.

It is interesting to note that Jesus did not appeal to legal authority to vindicate his teaching but to the knowledge he had learned from his Father. When accused of testifying on his own behalf, and thus invalidly, Jesus replied: 'Even if I am testifying to myself, my evidence is valid, for I know where I have come from and I know where I am going...I am one testifying to myself, and the second witness to me is the Father who sent me' (John 8.14, 18). Jesus goes on to say: 'I am only speaking to this world what I myself have heard from him [the Father]...I do nothing on my own authority but speak simply as my Father has taught me' (John 8.24, 28). In short, Jesus is a teacher *because* and *in so far as* he is a learner.

III Teaching and learning in the Asian tradition

Linking teaching with learning, and more precisely, making learning a condition for effective teaching, was not Jesus' practice alone. It was also that of Kongzi (or Kong Fuzi, Latinized as Confucius, 551–479 BCE), venerated as China's greatest teacher of wisdom, an ironic twist since Confucius was reluctant to accept the title of 'teacher' and did not advocate teaching as a profession.[2]

It is well-known that education is highly prized not only in China but in countries whose cultures have been shaped by the Confucian tradition, such as Japan, Korea, and Vietnam. For Confucius, education does not begin with the teacher but rather with the student, and the success of learning does not depend primarily on intellectual gifts but on the student's unquenchable desire to learn, without which all the teacher's labour, however skilful, would be in vain. Confucius himself embodies this thirst for learning: 'Even when walking in the company of two men, I am bound to find my teachers there. Their good points, I would try to emulate; their bad points, I would try to correct in myself.'[3] Note that Confucius did not say that he would try to correct the 'bad points' in others, but in himself, implying a process of learning from the mistakes of others.

There are three words in Chinese for 'teaching', each with its own distinctive nuance. *Hui* is teaching 'by way of imparting light'; *xun* is teaching 'by giving a lesson or a lecture'; and *jiao* is teaching by instruction, implying an unequal relationship between the superior instructor and the inferior instructed. Annping Chin notes that *xun* is not used in the *Analects*, the collection of Confucius's teaching, and that Confucius does not see himself – or any teacher for that matter – as performing *jiao*, for he sees the teacher not so much as superior to the learner but as engaged in the continual process of learning, as are the students.[4] Confucius sees the role of teaching as throwing light (*hui*) on one corner of the square: if a student does not come back with the other three (corners) after I have shown him one, I will not repeat what I have done.'[5] Indeed, Confucius insists that on the basis of his own insight a student has the right to contradict the teacher: 'When encountering matters that involve (the basic principles) of humanity, do not yield even to your teacher.'[6] Hence the importance of thinking, and, we may add, teaching and learning at the same time: 'If you simply learn but do not think, you will be bewildered. But if you simply think but do not learn, you will be in danger.'[7]

In short, for Confucius the teacher par excellence, life is a continual and unending process of learning. This is precisely how he sees his own life: 'At fifteen, I set my heart on learning. At thirty, I found my balance through the rites. At forty, I was free from doubts (about myself). At fifty, I understood what Heaven intended me to do. At sixty, I was attuned to what I heard. At seventy, I followed what my heart desired without overstepping the line.'[8]

Another teacher figure in the Asian tradition is highly relevant to the present theme of teaching as learning: the gurū (Sanskrit for 'heavy' or 'weighty').[9] In Hinduism the gurū is someone who is recognized by his or her disciple as having achieved liberation (*moksa*), that is, as having realized the non-duality between the self (*ātman*) and ultimate reality (*Brahman*). In virtue of this liberation, the gurū, and he or she alone, is able to lead others to this highest stage of self-realization. Often the gurū is venerated as 'god' by the disciple, but in fact, the guru does not achieve 'divinity' by himself or herself but becomes so by being acknowledged as such by the disciple.

It is to be noted that what qualifies the gurū as teacher is not only academic knowledge but personal self-realization, or 'dwelling entirely in Brahman', as the *Mundaka Upanisad* states: 'Nothing that is eternal (not made) can be gained by what is not eternal (made). Let him, in order to understand this, take fuel in his hand and approach a gurū who is learned and dwells entirely in Brahman' (1:2:12). For the disciple, the gurū is the way to liberation. In the *Maitrī Upanisad* the disciple addresses the gurū thus: 'In this world I am like a frog in a dry well. O saint, thou art my way, thou art my way' (1:4).

According to Śankara (788–820), the foremost exponent of Advaita Vedānta, the gurū, in order to be an effective teacher, must be free from 'deceit, pride, trickery, wickedness, fraud, jealousy, falsehood, egotism, [and] self interest' (*Upadeśsasāhasrī* 2:1:6). In *bhakti* [devotional] Hinduism, the primary role of the gurū is not only to teach but to show compassion and love toward the disciple. In the Tantric tradition, the gurū also initiates the disciple into the way of liberation. Finally, in the *Trika* or Kashmir Śaivism, the gurū's task is to awaken the spiritual energy (*kundalinī*) in the disciple for spiritual transformation. While the role of the gurū as a teacher is more active than that of the Confucian teacher and the gurū's liberation is seen as an achieved status, nevertheless the disciple is strongly warned against the danger of the false gurū: 'fools dwelling in darkness, wise in their own conceit, and puffed up with vain knowledge, (who) go round and round, staggering to and fro, like blind men led by the blind' (*Mundaka Upanisad*, 1:2:8). Thus, even for the gurū, authentic self-realization though continual spiritual practice is the *sine qua non* of effective teaching.

IV Bishops and Theologians as Learners and Teachers

Keeping in mind these reflections on Jesus the Teacher as obedient learner,

Confucius the Master as perpetual student, and the guru as one continually engaged in spiritual liberation, let us return to bishops and theologians as teachers of the faith. What are the implications of seeing teaching as learning for our understanding of what bishops and theologians teach, how they teach, and how they are related to one another?

As is widely acknowledged, bishops and theologians are teachers, but the grounds for their teaching authority are different. Bishops teach by virtue of their episcopal ordination which confers upon them both the ministry and the authority to teach in the name of Christ (*cathedra pastoralis*). Their teaching carries with it a certain legal power. By contrast, theologians teach by virtue of their acquired knowledge (*cathedra magisterialis*) –leaving out of consideration the question of the *mandatum*. Their teaching carries as much weight as their scholarly competence and has no canonical consequences.

While this distinction between the two *magisteria* is theologically accurate, its practical implications for effective teaching are doubtful. It is useful to recall that neither Jesus nor Confucius nor the guru based his teaching authority, and the veracity of his teachings, on juridical power, academic credentials, or scholarly competence. Instead, their claim to teach is based on their *personal experience* of what they teach and their *continual learning or hearing* of what they teach. They teach authoritatively precisely because they are attentive and obedient learners. What they teach is not validated by appeal to normative books, e.g., the Hebrew Bible, the classics, or philosophical treatises, although they respect these writings. Their teachings are based on what they have learned personally. In the same vein, it should be said that what bishops and theologians teach should not come primarily from ecumenical councils, catechisms, papal pronouncements, and Augustine, Thomas, Rahner, von Balthasar or Ratzinger, but should be deeply rooted in what they have personally learned. Teachers receive a sympathetic hearing from their students not because they repeat, possibly word-for-word, what is in the books, in virtue of their teaching office and duty, but because their students realize that they have appropriated in their lives what they teach. In other words, the students accept what their teachers teach because they perceive that the teachers personally know what they are talking about thanks to learning, and not because they have the power to do so. This is particularly true in areas where empirical evidence is in principle not available, such as those dealing with 'faith and morals', the proper province of church teaching. Appeal to authority in these cases betrays the lack of credible arguments. It is the perfect case of the emperor having no clothes.

Today, in the wake of the sex-abuse scandals and the way church authorities have dealt with them, the laity and the public at large may be forgiven for being highly suspicious of any claim on the part of the episcopal magisterium to teach authoritatively in moral matters. The reason is not that they deny bishops the right to teach. Rather they do not put faith in their teachings, because the teachers do not and seemingly refuse to *learn* – from experience, the sufferings of the victims, the voice of the faithful, the advice of the experts they themselves appointed, the courts, and the police. They teach but do not learn. They do not teach *as* learners. Their voice is not their own coming, as it should, from continual and assiduous learning, but functions merely as a voice-over of their ecclesiastical superiors. This is also true—*mutatis mutandis* – of theologians. These teachers tend to speak from bookish knowledge – the proverbial ivory tower –and are not immune from the danger of seeing themselves mainly as teachers (or better, 'professors' and 'doctors'), especially since their professional identity is canonically defined by the licence to teach 'in the name of the Church' (the *mandatum* granted by the local bishop, who – ironically enough – may not possess theological competence), and not by a constantly cultivated desire to learn.

Moreover, Jesus, as the Letter to the Hebrews reminds us, 'learned obedience through what he suffered'. This learning through suffering makes Jesus' teaching authentic and persuasive. His life was the price of what he learned. But popes, bishops and theologians usually do not follow this course. On the contrary, they are even awarded ecclesiastical or academic promotions for what they teach, especially when their teaching repeats the orthodox line, or what is fashionable in academic guilds. What they teach is derived from books and the *auctoritates*; they did not learn it in the school of suffering. No wonder their teaching does not carry much weight.

But how do you teach *as a learner*? Certainly not with threats of excommunication, *latae sententiae*, interdict, suspension, dismissal, notification, declaration, and an arsenal of other canonical weapons, nor, for theologians, with conferences, lecture circuits, and a stream of publications. Confucius's saying that a ruler who resorts to punishment shows that he has failed as a ruler can be applied equally to teachers. Jesus does not want to testify on his own behalf. Confucius refuses to be called teacher or master, and readily accepts being contradicted by his students. The guru's authority is established not by his or her own claim but by the recognition of the disciple. The teacher as learner does no more than, to cite Confucius again, throw light (*hui*) on one corner of the square, leaving the other three to discovery by the student. Like the guru's, the role of the teacher of the faith – bishops and theologians – is to set Christians on the path of knowledge and liberation, initiate them to their own journey of self-discovery, awaken spiritual energy – in Christian terms, the power of the Holy Spirit – in them, and not 'lecture' (*xun*) or 'instruct' (*jiao*) as one possessing superior knowledge and power. In other words, as teachers-learners, bishops and theologians must be first of all spiritual persons, and not purveyors of information, deeply aware that what they teach is not hallowed formulas and approved answers but the Divine Mystery, whom they must ceaselessly learn from, and before whom they kneel in adoring silence. Karl Rahner's remark that Christians in the future must be mystics, or Christianity will have no future, applies more than ever to the teachers of the Christian faith, bishops and theologians alike.

V   Relations between bishops and theologians

How should bishops and theologians relate to one another in the context of teaching learning? It may be useful to point out that the current model of the interaction between these two *magisteria* and the ways of conceiving their respective competencies are far from satisfactory. Not only is teaching separated from learning but the teaching function itself is regarded legalistically, as an exercise of power. One group of teachers, that is, the bishops, claims to possess authority over another group of teachers, that is, theologians, in virtue of their mysterious (magical?) charism of office – and not of superior knowledge and deeper insight resulting from assiduous learning and life-long spiritual discipleship. Furthermore, the teachings are treated as legal edicts to which assent and conformity are expected. No wonder that bishops (or worse, certain theologians appointed by them, whose scholarship is not universally or highly respected by their peers) are suspicious of theologians as potential rivals usurping their exclusive power to teach 'authentically', and on a perpetual lookout for 'theological dissidents' and 'ambiguities' in their writings. On the other hand, theologians are tempted to repay the compliment by looking upon bishops as bullies whose grasp of power far exceeds their intelligence.

How can this tension between the two kinds of teachers be alleviated if not eliminated? One possible way is for bishops and theologians to view themselves as learners, and more precisely, as *fellow learners*, in the company of both groups. The old adage that 'nobody ever learns anything while talking' can usefully be modified to read: 'while *teaching*'. But to be an intentional student is to be driven by a natural desire to learn. Furthermore, to be a student among other students does not mean that they must compete with each other but learning *with* and *from* others. It is not unusual for students to work together on a common research project, often with the teacher as a co-researcher who cannot carry the project to a successful end without the students' contributions. In this way, bishops and theologians teach each other by learning from each other, and learn from each other by teaching each other. The ecclesiology operative in this model of teaching as learning is that of the Church, not as a hierarchical structure of teachers versus learners – the *ecclesia docens* above the *ecclesia discerns* – but as a community of disciples equally engaged in the endless quest for knowledge through continuous learning together.

The goal of this learning is not mastery of information about matters of faith so that one can teach competently. Rather it is 'learned ignorance', to use the celebrated phrase from the work *De docta ignorantia* of the fifteenth-century Cardinal Nicholas of Cusa (1401–64). In his insightful introduction to *Learned Ignorance: Intellectual Humility among Jews, Christians, and Muslims* (2011), a collection of papers for a conference organized by the Institute for Advanced Catholic Studies, James Heft, SM, contrasts 'intellectual humility', which is an 'attitude of a thinker' with 'learned ignorance', which is 'the acknowledgment of religious believers that what they try to understand – namely God, and the ways of God – constantly transcends their ability to grasp fully and articulate adequately what they have experienced.'[10] Replace 'thinker' with 'learner', 'religious believers' with 'theologians and bishops', and 'understand' with 'learn', and the point of this essay is made.

It is possible to object that this thesis about teaching as learning will lead to relativism and despair about ever arriving at the truth, and thus deprive church authorities of the power to teach. One contributor to the above-mentioned volume, David Burrell, notes this danger and replies that teaching about faith is not offering 'explanations' of statements of faith. Statements of faith, he points out, are 'convictions': 'Convictions that there is a sense to it all; not that we can make sense of it all. What fuels that conviction is one's growing capacity to use a language which helps us progressively gain our bearings in the midst of a journey.'[11] But how can bishops and theologians, too preoccupied with teaching as they are, find their bearings in the midst of their journeys of faith if they do not constantly learn?

Are all these reflections on teaching as learning too idealistic for the conflict-laden relation between theologians and bishops? If the workings of Asian bishops and theologians in the Federation of Asian Bishops' Conferences are any guide, there is good evidence that my proposals are not naive and impractical lucubrations but have animated relations between Asian bishops and Asian theologians over the last 30 years.[12]

But we need not go so far as Asia to see how these reflections on teaching as learning work. Those of us who grew into adulthood in the 1980s remember with nostalgia how the bishops of the United States were engaged in a collective process of learning as they drew up their pastoral letters on peace and the economy. More personally, that bishop who invited me, a theological novice back in 1988, to help him understand contemporary theological developments, could have invoked his episcopal magisterium but did not. He wished to learn, and in so doing he taught me more than he could ever imagine, and in 'teaching' him, I learned more than I could ever imagine.

Notes

1. See Francis Sullivan, *Magisterium: Teaching Authority in the Catholic Church*, New York, 1983; id., *Creative Fidelity: Weighting and Interpreting Documents of the Magisterium*, New York, 1996; Ladislas Örsy, *The Church: Teaching and Learning*, Wilmington, DE, 1987; Thomas Rausch, *Authority and Leadership in the Church: Past Directions and Future Possibilities*, Wilmington, DE, 1989; Richard Gaillardetz, *Witnesses to the Faith: Community, Infallibility, and the Ordinary Magisterium of Bishops*, New York, 1992; id., *Teaching with Authority: A Theology of the Magisterium in the Church*, Collegeville, MN, 1997; id., *By What Authority? A Primer on Scripture, the Magisterium, and the Sense of the Faithful*, Collegeville, MN, 2003.
2. For an informative exposition on Confucius as a teacher, see Annping Chin, *The Authentic Confucius: A Life of Thought and Politics*, New York, 2007, pp. 142–71.
3. Annping Chin, *The Authentic Confucius, op. cit.*, pp. 143–4.
4. *Ibid.*, p. 147.
5. *Ibid.*, p. 144.
6. *Ibid.*, p. 145.
7. *Ibid.*, p. 149.
8. *Ibid.*, p. 171.
9. On the guru, especially in comparison with Christianity, see Catherine Cornille, *The*

Guru in Indian Catholicism: Ambiguity or Opportunity of Inculturation?, Louvain, 1991.
10. James L. Heft, Reuven Firestone & Omid Safi (eds), *Learned Ignorance: Intellectual Humility among Jews, Christians, and Muslims*, Oxford, 2011, p. 4.
11. David Burrell, *Faith and Freedom: An Interfaith Perspective*, Oxford, 2001, p. 245.
12. On the work of the Theological Advisory Commission of the FABC, later renamed the Office of Theological Concerns, see Vimal Tirimanna (ed.), *Harvesting from the Asian Soil: Toward an Asian Theology*, St Mary's Town, Bangalore, 2011.

Part Two: Theological Forum

Introduction: Silence in the Church

We have chosen a different form for the Theological Forum in this issue of *Concilium*. The topic is one that we find profoundly disturbing.

The Catholic Church has been shaken by scandals. The most shocking of these is the sexual violence which priests and others have practised, or which has occurred in church contexts, or both. In 2004, *Concilium* devoted an issue to the theme of structural betrayal of trust and sexual abuse in the Church. But we can also observe forms of abuse at other levels in the Church: abuse of office and power, discrimination as abuse of the message of liberation, and abuse of the Gospel by leaving the marginalized where they are and putting one's own position or institution to the fore.

All these forms of abuse have something in common: they all depend on a particular kind of silence. This is saying nothing in order to make the structure and the institution more important than people. It is saying nothing in order to put your own reputation, your own welfare or your own superiority above telling the truth. It is a form of silence that not only says nothing but tells lies.

This refusal to speak out can be an inward silence accompanied by a lot of outward talk, so that nothing is said about what is going on inside the Church but moral judgements on 'the world' outside are always forthcoming. It can also be an outward silence accompanied by a lot of inward talk, for instance when a political judgement is avoided in the presence of injustice, constraint, or inhumanity, whereas a strict moral code is imposed on individual believers.

In some contexts this silence may be so deeply engraved in one's own identity that it has become second nature. Securing one's identity by holding on to power at all costs leads inevitably to blind spots.

The following texts are about silence and truth telling in the Church. They come from Brazil, Canada and Croatia. Their specific contexts lead to questions about the Church's real duty of speaking out and telling the truth.

The forum proper is followed by an interview with the church historian Hubert Wolf about Pius XII and the process for his beatification that has distressed many people inside and outside the Church, especially because of Pius XII's attitude to the Nazi persecution of the Jews.

Relations between Truth, Authority, Power and Sacredness in the Church

LUIZ CARLOS SUSIN

At the heart of the problem of non-recognized abuse – abuse of various sorts, sexual, intellectual, moral, spiritual – may lie the question of the 'sacred'. This is an issue that involves both people and the institution in a religious domain composed of 'sacred' elements, 'Christian sacredness', even after the whole modern critique of the sacred. It is part of the Church's doctrine and practice to consider the hierarchy as an order endowed with sacred powers by divine revelation since the New Testament (cf. Vatican II, *Lumen Gentium*, 18ff). But in the face of proven abuses it publicly recognizes its mistake or ignorance and apologizes. Is it still really 'sacred'? This is a complex question and simple answers do not do justice to complex questions. From the start we must resist the temptation to dualistic, especially Manicheistic, solutions: in this case legitimate institutional power, with recognized authority, is a necessity for life in society, and this applies to the Church too. In the case of a Christian Church there are three levels that can be usefully distinguished (but not separated): the Gospel, the religious and the sacred. I will deal mainly with the third.

I The Gospel of truth and the debate about authority and power

From the point of view of Jesus as he is remembered, it is easy to recognize, on the one hand, his charismatic authority in the best theological sense of the term: his *exousia* as bearer of the Father's Spirit. On the other hand, this authority and power were exercised on behalf of truth in a prophetic way, in tension and contrast with the powers of this world and the sacred power deriving from the Temple and the Law. Jesus before Pilate in John 19 and in his criticisms of religion with reference to the

Temple in Matthew 23 are trenchant examples: he questions authority and power.

Jesus' attitude to the exercise of authority and power is well known: it is first of all an exercise of service, of care and healing, and only in this context of *kenosis* also authority and power to teach. But the New Testament is also the time after Easter, the time of the Christian communities who need authorities to refer to and to govern them, pastors to be a model for the flock. The New Testament itself does not hide the tensions between the novelty of Jesus and the need for some continuity with tradition and for some emerging hierarchical institutions.

II The institution of the religious dimension, truth and *interpretations*

Without separating faith and religion, or even Gospel and religion, it is important to accept the distinction: *religion* is a *human* expression of faith and the Gospel. Religion is structured in terms of community, society and culture. What is valid for other religious traditions is also valid for Christianity, in the sense that historically the Gospel became the Christian *religion*. Doctrines, dogmas, discipline of behaviour and thinking, rituals and hierarchy, are all essential elements of religion. And it is in religion that hierarchy becomes more complex, more legal and more dogmatic, marking out frontiers and identities.

Christianity, as it became religion and culture, shared the glories and conflicts of religions, but maintained the golden thread of the Gospel that is also a criterion and critique of religion, including of itself as religion. Today the cultural basis of the 'Christian' West is autonomy, the horizontal relationships of democracy and respect for freedom of religion. The Gospel can take some credit for being the historical root of these values. Appeal to a sacred authority, by 'divine right', via metaphysical reasoning or a founding narrative is no longer sufficient or plausible justification. It is judged by its fruits, its actions.

An important contribution to solving the crisis of authority, and therefore of power, is to put into practice the Church's missionary and servant role, the test of love. This would reveal in all its clarity the Gospel as the source of authority and power, Christian 'sacredness'. But for our present purposes we need to go deeper and examine the tendency to sacralize religious power and the consequences of this.

III The sacralization of power, obscuring reality and its victims

The 'sacred' sounds like an untouchable mystery that requires no justification. There are different ways of unpacking this concept. Here I shall make a distinction between the 'holy', the 'religious' and the 'sacred'. I shall use 'sacred' in the anthropological sense, the *tremendum et fascinans*, which creates the necessity for *sacrifices* and *taboos*, or, in more modern terms, *surrender* and *limit*. This includes surrender and limitation of reason, of will and behaviour, where rights become subordinate to the mystery of the sacred. This brings us to the 'archaic sacredness' and the *Homo Sacer* of Giorgio Agamben's studies, where the exception has authority over the rule and becomes a rule that suspends the rule. This makes sense of the absolutism that rooted itself in divine power and gave rise to Hobbes' axiom: *auctoritas, non veritas, facit legem*. This authority needs to merge with sacredness without delegation in such a way that *Princeps legibus solutus est*. The principle – and the prince – is the creator of the law and remains above the law. Here there is a reversal of the relation between truth and authority: what authority establishes becomes truth, a principle with a nominalist flavour to preserve divine freedom from the objectivity of truth. In human historical and cultural conditions, and in the human exercise of authority, this strictly theological principle can become devastating. We recognize this from the symptoms.

One of the symptoms of this dangerous reversal of the logic of authority and power, intended to be guarantees of truth, is the appeal to sacredness to erect a strict separation between the power elite and the subjects. A hierarchy – from the village priest upwards – that is convinced that it is accountable only to God, and not to its people and their pleas or rights, and uses sacred arguments to justify this position, even quoting the Gospel, is an elite that cloaks itself in sacredness and obscures both truth and holiness. Elite and 'clergy' – the select portion – can fall here into an extremely problematic situation, which becomes a trap for the very people encapsulated and hardened within it. Allow me a personal recollection here. In 1980, in a discussion with Yves Congar, Congar asked me to take the Code of Canon Law and open it at the first canon on the rights of the laity – the right to have the means of salvation. He asked me how it was possible to let many of Latin America's Catholics slip into a form of Christianity that we criticized the Protestants for, Word without Eucharist? Today, 30 years later, the effects are indeed devastating, including for a clergy exhausted in the face of an increasingly Pentecostal Latin America. But, Congar concluded, the sacredness adopted by the hierarchy prevents any change.

Another symptom is the sacred secret. A secret that can make the clergy 'martyrs' to individual confession in today's culture is revealed as a matter of course to therapists, who may be married men or women. But the secret becomes a real problem in the exercise of ecclesiastical power. The secret consultations *sub gravi* for the appointment of bishops, the politics that refuses to admit that it is politics, in short, action in secret, even in good conscience, to govern and decide, allows for possible favouritism and, more generally, obscures what should be transparent processes. Clearly there are situations, in education, or where there are reasons of prudence or compassion, that justify secrecy, but when there is a systematic practice, justifying itself in terms of its own sacredness, it is practically impossible to avoid abuse.

Another symptom is the treatment of issues *inter pares*, with no direct reference to the people involved. This affects both different positions within the hierarchy and the relationship of the hierarchy with the laity. In the Church this typically feudal attitude, with very stubborn anthropological roots, affects 'ordinary priests', but also – and much more – the 'ordinary faithful'. There is a correlation of dignities that, at least indirectly, expels those who are at the bottom because, in a vertical structure, they enjoy less dignity. This may happen with the good intention of keeping the truth from the laity, for example, in order not to scandalize them. But there is also the contrary effect: the downplaying of the protests or simply the voice of the laity. There is no mutual learning, no reciprocity, no giving and receiving. What comes from above is unquestionable. Again I shall take the liberty of sharing a recollection. At the beginning of the 1990s the philosopher Enrique Dussel was warning us of the need to make a careful study of Canon Law. He argued that the euphoria that filled the Church, and the West, at the fall of the Socialist system, together with the exalted view the new spiritual movements held of Roman power, could open the door to decisions that violated Canon Law.

Another symptom is the hardening and the distortions of communications, because the sacredness we are talking about, instead of displaying the truth in all its splendour, obscures it. This produces not only out-of-date information and channels of communication poisoned by feudal stratification and by the policies of those who have access to them to the detriment of those who don't, but also apparently inexplicable surprises like the case of the Lefèbvrist bishop, Richard Williamson, who was a Holocaust denier, and the sad and unbelievable career of Marcial Maciel. Difficulties such as those faced by the diocese of Toowoomba in Australia and by the Vicariate of Sucumbíos in Ecuador were also aggravated by inadequate forms of communication. In any institution a heavily hierarchical structure makes it difficult to have objective and up-to-date communication, but this is increased in institutions that accentuate their sacred character and imagine that they are protected by impregnable walls. These very walls exact their price in a lack of real communication.

Finally, another symptom is the difficulty for conscience to remain the final sanctuary of discernment and responsibility when it is involved in the sacralization of an institution. The sacredness of conscience also has its limits and its need for education, but it is the final authority, as demonstrated by the witness of Thomas More and John Henry Newman, and by countless martyrs for conscientious convictions. Even if the ultimate authority of conscience over the most sacred of institutions is recognized doctrine, in practice it is difficult for a sacred institution to respect: it tends to make martyrs or crush and violate consciences, because not everyone has the good fortune to be allowed an *eppur si muove* position like Galileo, who, after all, was a friend of the Pope's.

In conclusion, first, independently of the people who are part of the hierarchy in good faith and with good intentions, hierarchy tends to produce victims of abuse of power precisely because it is *sacralized*. It tends to cover up the victimhood of the victims and make it invisible. Secondly, the victims are often made to take the blame. They become precisely the scapegoats whom the sacred needs as food. Finally something perverse happens when authority, instead of following the path of truth to obtain power, becomes the path of power for truth because of the sacralization of power. Perhaps this is an invincible narcissism.

Some time ago at a priestly ordination, I saw the newly ordained priest, after his hands had been anointed, invited to raise them and process round the church to applause and general reverence: *tremendum et fascinans*? More recently, I visited some colleagues working in the interior of tormented Haiti. And discreetly I noticed that one of them had calloused hands and nails he could never get quite clean because he had been digging wells with the people. I confess I wanted to kiss those hands: a 'Christian' *tremendum et fascinans*.

The truth that sets us free and gives us power has authority in the most basic etymological sense of the word – authority from the Latin *augere*, a care that makes us grow, 'truth as author' that sets us on the path of life, redefines power. Truth and power, in the last analysis, live together in love. Augustine saw the *tertium non datur* in the tough reconciliation between reason and faith, in the third element that generates and brings them together, love. The same can be said of the relation of truth and power: it is the third element, love, over and above all dialectic, that can save truth and power from brutishness. Love is the truth and authority with power, power to heal, free, teach and govern. Love is the holiness that counts in the end. With *Caritas in Veritate*, we also need to insist: *Veritas – et auctoritas et potestas – in Caritate.*

Translated by Francis McDonagh

Terrifying Internal Problems
What Theology Has to Say about Lies

SOLANGE LEFEBVRE

The first part of the title cites the words used by Pope Benedict XVI on his way to Portugal in May 2010, when he said that the scandal of sexual abuse committed by priests and religious 'does not come from outside enemies but is born of sin within the Church'. But which sin? The sin of pedophilia, of course, of abuse of minors by those in a position of power, but also, we would add, that of resorting to telling lies in order to avoid scandal. This ecclesiastical practice has a long history and was inspired by such suggestions as that of St Jerome: 'The second remedy after shipwreck is to hide one's sin...lest...others be scandalized thereby'.[2] The significance of the word 'scandal' here is important. Traditionally, it is derived from the Greek *skandalon*, which means a snare, or stumbling-block, and giving cause for scandal means carrying out an action or causing an event which is thought to be morally or legally wrong and provokes general public outrage.[3] There is also the later, probably twelfth-century, acceptation of 'scandal' (from Middle English, Old French and the ecclesiastical Latin *scandalum*), which refers to the public shock and anger caused by the reprehensible behaviour of a religious person. The Church has tended to cultivate the art or device of lying or dissimulation in order to preserve the reputation of the Church and of the individuals committing the sins in question. All the standard or traditional commentators on this theme recognize that certain lies are necessary or represent a lesser evil.

Benedict thought it necessary to refer to the internal nature of responsibility, in view of instances of strong resistance to the denunciation of, and ruthless dealing with, sexual abuse by religious. These internal problems surely include the way in which the abuse of minors and children has been all but trivialized. It is noteworthy that it was mentioned in the Universal Catechism of 1992, in the paragraph dealing with rape by members of the family (incest) or educators, under the heading 'Offences against Chastity' (par. 2356). Once it was reduced to the level of a sexual misdemeanour, the only way to treat this behaviour was forgiveness followed by dissimulation. In this respect, on the other hand, the competent secular authorities can hardly be said to have been any more perceptive. This is especially true of psychiatrists and social workers.

Disturbed by the scandalous cases of sexual abuse that have come to light, different Catholic tendencies have been inclined to pass the buck to one another. Liberal Catholics accuse the clergy of abusing their power and of a fraught understanding and treatment of sex, and attack the structure of the Church itself. Conservative Catholics attribute this aberrant behaviour of pedophile priests, and that of homosexuals involved in the abuse of minors, to the disarray of post-1968 societies, to wayward moral theologians, and to slack ecclesiastical discipline. If we add the claims of a lack of insight on the part of psychiatrists and social services, the trivialization of the Church's internal responsibility is at its height.

Theologically and with regard to discipline, it would seem necessary to treat lies and hypocrisy more seriously. These two themes have a very minimal place in our theological tradition, except as mere headings in works on morals and ethics. If you take the trouble to research the term 'lies' in theological indexes, you will find very little there. Yet one of the major commandments is about lying and bearing false witness, and evil is associated with an aboriginal lie, for the 'Devil', for instance, was known as the 'Father of lies' (John 8.44). Basic texts often combine and associate the duality of good and evil with that of truth and lies. In a sense, lying might be said to be the heart of evil. But what do we find in the main work of reference on disciplinary matters in the Church, the Code of Canon Law? The 1983 index to the Code cites lying at only two points. The first has to do with the usurpation of ecclesiastical offices, and uses the verb 'feign'. 'Feigning' the administration of a sacrament is prohibited (No. 1379). The second concerns the 'crime of falsification' in the case of a confirmed falsification in a public ecclesiastical document (No. 1391). That appears to sum up lies.

But the term 'scandal' leads us to a more fruitful outcome, for it is used almost twenty times in the section on criminal law. Par. 1318 is enlightening: 'The legislator will not threaten to apply penalties *latae sententiae* (automatic penalties) unless possibly for certain exceptionally mischievous offences which could give rise to serious scandal...'. Here we come across the two abovementioned acceptations of 'scandal': to cause to sin, and to cause outrage as far as public opinion is concerned. This accords with the thesis of the American theologians Thomas Doyle, Richard Sipe and Patrick Wall in their *Sex, Priests, and Secret Codes: The Catholic Church's 2,000-Year Paper Trail of Sexual Abuse*.[4] They maintain that secrecy and lies constitute a secular political *habitus*, or habitual tendency, on the part of the clergy when faced with the theological and canonical requirement to avoid scandal.[5] The Church has practised dissimulation of aberrant sexual behaviour by its members for centuries, even with regard to the abuse of children and minors, whatever conservative Catholics may say who attribute these aberrancies to the sexual revolution of the 1960s. A revision of the Church's penal law as embodied in the Code of Canon Law is in progress. We shall see how far it takes account of these grave problems.

Another absent topic is that of 'hypocrisy', although this was central to Jesus' criticism of religion. You will search in vain for any mention of hypocrisy in the fundamental manuals of the Christian faith. How has it become so minor a topic, even in dictionaries of usage and theological thought? Yet it is at the heart of Jesus's critique of religious authorities in the New Testament for simulated virtue and dissimulating perversity under the guise of outwardly virtuous religious practices. Hypocrites seek to deceive others and to obtain their approbation by a wholly external practice of religious gestures or merely apparent demonstrations of virtue. In Canada, the most recent example is that of the Bishop of the Catholic diocese of Antigonish, Raymond Lahey. Ironically, after having acted as a credible mediator between victims of sexual abuse and his diocese, he was arrested in an airport. He aroused suspicion as a frequent traveller to southeastern Asian countries, and a large number of child-porn photos were found on his computer. Was he sick? Certainly, as far as psychiatrists are concerned, but he was also a past master of the practice of lies and hypocrisy.

You are struck by the extreme existential anxiety of the philosopher Jean-Jacques Rousseau on reading his *Rêveries du promeneur solitaire* (The Reveries of a Solitary Walker, 1782), in which he follows Plutarch in discussing lying and describes his moral aversion to it. This is also apparent in Augustine, who wrote the first known theological treatise on lies, the *Contra mendacium* (Against lying), in which he concludes that lying is never an acceptable choice. In so doing one might protect someone from a physical threat, for example, but that is nothing compared with the injury inflicted on one's soul. Of eight possible degrees of falsehood, the most serious for Augustine has to do with doctrine, and the second with a lie which is pronounced to the detriment of a third party, and to no one's advantage (sections 9 to 24 of the treatise). In modern times, it would seem to be philosophers such as Kant, Nietzsche and Derrida who are more interested in lies.

Can we speak of a widespread repression of these questions in our tradition? To save face, a family, institution or group dissimulates the truth, and even denies it. When telling the truth about the hypocrisy of religious authorities, Jesus expressed a dangerous truth, which is related forthrightly in Matthew 23: 'Alas for you, you hypocritical scribes and Pharisees! You are like white-washed tombs, which look fine on the outside but inside are full of dead men's bones and all kinds of rottenness'. The Catholic Church is now obliged to undertake a radical revision of these practices of dissimulation, especially in respect of sexual behaviour. Our egalitarian and democratic societies have developed an acute sense of personal dignity, call for more exacting accounts from their leaders and administrators, and, more profoundly, are in the process of desacralizing authorities that had been unassailable until that point. The scandal now is to refuse to get at the truth and tell it. It could be that doing precisely this, quite beyond the denunciation of pedophile crimes, will even lead Catholicism to admit that it is incapable of effectively controlling the sexual behaviour of the vast number of its members who have taken a vow of celibacy, a practice which the Church has surely generalized to the point of excess.

Translated by J. G. Cumming

Notes

1. The title echoes Benedict XVI's remarks as reported by the media when he was on his way to Portugal in May 2010. He was said to have spoken about internal problems in the Church which we now witness in a 'truly terrifying way': 'Today we see in a truly terrifying way that the greatest persecution of the Church does not come from outside enemies but is born of sin within the Church.' Cf. http://www.rtl.fr/actualites/article/pedophilie-dans-l-eglise-benoit-xvi-evoque-une-verite-terrifiante-5940389564.
2. Quoted in Thomas Aquinas, *Summa Theologica* (vol. 2, London & New York, 1947, pp.1669–70), 'Of Dissimulation and Hypocrisy', Question 111, First Article: '[a man] dissembles not if he omits to signify what he is. Hence one may hide one's sin without being guilty of dissimulation. It is thus that we must understand the saying of Jerome on the words of Isaiah (3.9; 16.14) that the second remedy after shipwreck is to hide one's sin, lest, to wit, others be scandalized thereby.'
3. Leviticus 19.14; Mark 9.12. Thomas Aquinas, *Summa Theologica, op. cit. supra*, pp. 1366–73), 'Of Scandal', Question 43, First Article.

4. T. Doyle, R. Sipe & P. Wall, *Sex, Priests, and Secret Codes: The Catholic Church's 2,000-Year Paper Trail of Sexual Abuse*, Los Angeles, 2006. A few other works on this subject recently mention the question of lies and hypocrisy, for instance J. Berry & G. Renner, *Vows of Silence: The Abuse of Power in the Papacy of John Paul II*, New York, London, Toronto & Sydney, 2004.
5. It should be remarked that paragraphs 1394 and 1395 of the Code of Canon Law refer to scandal in the traditional sense of causing someone else to fall into sin, and recommend that the clerical status of abusers should be terminated.

Silence and Concealment in the Church in Croatia

FRANO PRCELA OP

You don't have to be a member or close confidant of the Catholic hierarchy, or even play an especially committed part in the everyday life of the Church, to be in a position to cite at least a few of the more important topics or challenges about which the Church would rather say nothing. Nevertheless, I don't see my task in this article as one of addressing taboo themes, and I certainly don't intend to act as a kind of voyeur displaying the Church's 'dirty washing' for the contemplation of a wider public. Instead I want to try to answer the question: Why does the Church keep quiet when it ought to speak out? And the further question: How can it continue to say nothing when public opinion, and not merely the Catholic public, not only expects it to speak but even more to show integrity, sincerity and selfless commitment? If we start from the assumption that silence does not consist merely of a failure to talk, we are forced to ask what are the real consequences of the Church's silence, not only for the future view of the Church in Croatian society, but especially for its primary mission: the proclamation of the Good News.

I Elucidations and illustrations

First, I have to make a few points that are variously relevant to the theme of silence and concealment in the Church. The very theme needs some elucidation. Silence or concealment in the Church does not necessarily refer only to a lack of public pronouncements by the Church about its own problems, but to its saying nothing about social problems. It is a question not only of silence about what is going on inside the Church but one that has to do with the presence of the Church in society. They both have to be taken into account: the domestic silence of the Church and the silence of the Church in public (opinion) in Croatia.

Second, the Catholic Church in Croatia is not only an immense and ineradicable presence in Croatian society in a statistical sense (almost 90 per cent of the citizens of the Republic of Croatia are formally members of the Catholic Church), but the respect in which it is held also makes it an extremely influential institution in society, and therefore also an important factor in decision processes, and with regard to subjects that are significant for Croatian society. But powerful institutions by their nature are economical with their pronouncements when self-criticism is at issue. That is not only true of the Catholic Church in Croatia.

Third, we have to remember that during the Communist dictatorship (1945–90), because of circumstances that were highly unfavourable to the Church, it was forced to submit to a self-imposed 'inner silence'. Disempowered and restricted to an extremely limited sphere of action, it could not risk venturing on a public life calling for any greater impetus than it could afford then. Consequently, the Church avoided saying anything about internal problems in order to focus all permissible efforts on combating its overwhelmingly powerful ideological enemy. Therefore it tried to appear like a harmonious and united institution externally, while seeking to avoid internal conflicts at any price.[1]

Fourth, under Communism the Church was repressed to the point of dwelling 'in the sacristy'. With the introduction of democratic changes, the doors to public opinion were thrown wide open, an opportunity which the Church used not only without any forethought, but often quite injudiciously. To make matters worse, in any attempt to initiate public discussion at that time, Croatian society had to bear the burden of the tragic experience of war (1991–5), which also brought the Church to the fore as an instance of consolation and relief. During the war the Church performed quite well in the sphere of humanitarian and pastoral care and aid, but neglected itself in the process. Borne forward by the strength of its self-image as an unquestioned national authority and powerful institution, it did not see the need to prepare for a pluralist society and growing secularization.

These introductory remarks are important if we are to reach any understanding of the present silence of the Church and of silence in the Church.

II Living in a state of contradiction

Even in Communist Yugoslavia, Croatia had an independent political movement, the so-called 'Croat Spring', which advocated political change.

But like many other similar movements in Communist countries behind the Iron Curtain, the 'Croat Spring' was suddenly stopped in its tracks in the early 1970s. The Croat Communist leadership was violently replaced, and the leaders of the student movement and many intellectuals were gaoled for many years. This was followed by what was subsequently known as the 'Croat silence'. Nevertheless, the Church remained the only voice of real significance speaking up for the interests of the Croat nation.

Supported by its centuries-old experience as guardian of Croat national and cultural identity, the Church continued to play an extremely active and inclusive role in the nation, even after the democratic changes of the 1990s.[2] In the existential experience of people who saw themselves as compelled to wage defensive war, the Church bore the heavy burden of relieving the wounds inflicted during the war as well as the associated suffering. This raised its popular reputation to its highest point. Yet expectations exceeded any possibility of their fulfilment. The confusion of war delayed attempts to deal with urgent tasks pressing on the young democracy: repairing the crimes of the Communist era, a basic elucidation of the recent past, the construction of democratic media, and the provision of a genuinely civil society. With the introduction of an independent State liberated from Serbian occupation, the political and social setting has been in a state of constant destabilization right up to the present.

The Catholic hierarchy also continually reminds those holding posts of responsibility in the Croatian State that the national interests are still disregarded to a degree that endangers the security of the State, so far so that there must be a definite end to the 'Croat silence'.[3] In essence, of course, this is far from undesirable, but the real problem is that this emphatically political initiative comes from the Catholic hierarchy. For some years now, the episcopal messages on high feast days (Easter, the Assumption or Christmas) have taken the form of politological analyses or diagnoses and political recommendations. This means that the Church remains silent within by failing to promote a more active basic religious education of the faithful,[4] yet openly announces what it wants from the political and social establishment in a familiar ecclesiastical setting.[5]

III Motes and beams

If, as I have noted, the Catholic hierarchy overstresses national themes and ethnic rhetoric in the existing circumstances of democratic life and work, it is not surprising that there is such a lack of creative pastoral initiative and appropriately contemporary theological analysis.[6] Under such conditions, a highly-traditional Catholicism accelerates the Church's contraction to the status of a liturgical community and its prophetic voice becomes mere social criticism. Admittedly, under special conditions, like those that existed when Croatia was attacked, it was wholly appropriate to concentrate on questions concerning the nation and State. On the other hand, under normal democratic conditions of political action, the Church's primary task cannot be that of a political spokesman. Yet an impartial observer might easily suppose that the Catholic Church in Croatia was nationally or even nationalistically inclined. Ultimately, however, what the Church has to say about national problems, where the emphasis recently has been increasingly on questions of the State as such, is not a nationalistic discourse, but rather a discussion and conversation prompted by the Church's fear of losing its privileged position in State and society. Unfortunately, by addressing 'its people' and concerning itself with their political topics, the Church, *nolens volens*, chooses a fatal path. To a certain extent, it neglects its faithful, and might even be said to desert them, although they ought to be its primary addressees and primary substance. In so doing it not only changes its substance but its role. By imitating what is proper to others, it splits its own community, and gives rise to a dichotomy, or 'schism', between the institution and lived faith. If, in political discussions, the 'increment' of the institution's argument put forward on the basis of authority (often unconsciously) forces the authority of argument into the background, the situation becomes totally confused. Public political debate in the Church may occasionally succeed in breaking the 'Croat silence', but the change that has taken place in themes and roles leads to a shift in the priorities of the Church's own specific mission. This paradox encourages the erosion of the Church's pastoral efficacy and thoroughly obscures the proclamation of the Gospel proper to it.

IV Dealing with criticism

How does the Church react to the criticism directed against it? When trying to answer this question it is important not to forget that the regime in Tito's Yugoslavia categorically rejected all critical comments from the Catholic Church with regard to the Socialist reality of that period and took no notice of even the most commonplace objections to specific social phenomena.

The Communist rulers refused to allow the Church any kind of participation in discussion, claiming that this would mean it was interfering in political affairs and thereby venturing on forbidden ground. Representatives of the Catholic hierarchy tried to back up their statements with relevant arguments, but they never succeeded in doing more than knock on closed doors. As far as the regime was concerned, public life was the canonically reserved territory of the Communist Party, where the Church was forbidden to trespass.

Nowadays, when they have to deal with criticism of the Church, representatives of the hierarchy appear to behave just like the former Communist rulers. They hasten to bring public debate to an end with pro and contra arguments, in order to put the critic or opponent in an ideological corner as quickly as possible. Criticism is far too readily treated as an attack on the Church. Although certain media publish expressly ill-intentioned and untrue statements about the Church, above all recently, that does not justify church representatives doing their best to ensure that necessary discussions degenerate to the level of an ideological squabble. The Catholic Church has to learn to suffer fierce criticism gladly. Of course this criticism has often been quite dangerous, and for some people absolutely lethal, as it certainly was for Blessed Cardinal Alojzije Stepinac and the many priests either executed or sentenced to many years of penal servitude after World War II. But the Catholic hierarchy seems to cling to its traditional reticence even under the conditions of a politically liberal State, and to be unable to enter into peaceful and constructive dialogue with secular society in Croatia.[7] Why does it still behave like this?

Of course the Church can seem very loquacious and eloquent in its social manifestation. It is quite willing to define its teachings and advocate morally correct behaviour. It is scarcely slow to correct contrary opinions and proclaims its viewpoint with *ex cathedra* fluency and persuasiveness. But it is not interested in confronting other viewpoints. Usually it does not go beyond statements and communiqués, and sometimes even seems to be intent indirectly on advising its partner in dialogue of the need to 'convert' (to the sole authentic outlook). It doesn't seem interested in encounter with, and intellectual apprehension and contextual understanding of, those who think differently, but is mainly concerned to get anyone with another viewpoint to realize where the solution is actually to be found. It is not only that there is no confrontation with contrary opinions in the Church: it doesn't even show any interest in verifying its own standpoints. If there is a scandal in the Church and individual office-holders upset the basis of the trust shown in the institution, then the Church says nothing. Civic and public opinion (including that of the faithful) is informed mainly by public media, whereas when 'bad news' about the Church is in question, its official representatives only start talking when everything the official Church should have said long before has already emerged. Furthermore, they offer excuses only if no other course remains open to them, and solely to limit the harm done to the reputation of the institution.[8] At long last the Church shows candour. But the candour is forced.

If the reputation of the institution is endangered, rapid action is the chosen course, whereas if the threat concerns truth in the Church or the truth about the Church, then they hold back, take the measure of the situation, try to win time, and hide things. They even go so far as to directly prohibit any statement whatsoever, lest the truth should be revealed. This happened recently in the 'Dajla' case', when there was a dispute about legal ownership in a Benedictine monastery in Istria. In general the Church categorically rejects any public criticism or just remains impervious to it. The result of this significant silence is ever more frequent 'debates', or public discussions about the Church but without the Church, which are (not only but for the most part) highly injurious to the Church.

V Existing without its own public opinion

The Catholic hierarchy behaves as described in respect of criticism from outside, because that is exactly its attitude to its own communications within the Church. Mistrust of talk around the table of Croat public opinion is powered by the fact that there is still no internal public opinion within the Church. Of course, there are attempts at dialogue inside the Church, but they seem to have little or no value as communication. Furthermore, what purpose can such conversations have other than to help keep the institution going? The institution's good reputation? The personal prestige of certain individuals? Dialogue for truth's sake? Then there is the ultimate question: Where is truthful communication in which actions and words agree? The Catholic hierarchy is essentially concerned to present the Church outwardly and inwardly as an institution which is united and harmonious in its own right. This concern is both legitimate and understandable. But there is a price to pay for this, which seems to be 'any price'. If you want to achieve unity at any price, very soon you resort to a uniform way of thinking. When harmony is imposed, you no longer hear anything of different or (God forbid!) contrary viewpoints, and too much emphasis on tradition leads to the suppression of creativity. As a result the Church could very soon find itself on the very dangerous ground where all it really seems interested in is defending its own prescriptions and its own reputation at any price. Then obedience is demanded but not the exercise of responsibility, and individual conscience is sacrificed for the sake of the institution's reputation. This is good neither for the institution nor for its future and authenticity.

In this split situation, religious, priests and bishops as well as church officials (which means lay-people too) have to decide between the institution and their own conscience, and incline far too readily to so-called obedience, which means that they decide not to follow their own conscience. The result of this kind of (non-)communication is not untrammelled talk and discussion but complaisance, evasion and silence. They don't say what they think but what their superior wants to hear and whatever serves the purposes of their own career.[9] Voicing any kind of criticism under such conditions must seem tantamount to disloyalty.

If there is no possibility of open disagreement, problems are not raised but tucked away out of sight, and there is neither discussion nor publicity. Uniform concealment is indifferent to criticism, and a conflict of opinions is only possible in secret. In these circumstances the Church maintains a demonstrative yet strained presence in public and continues to exist without its own primary public opinion. Of course, the Church shouldn't divulge everything about its own affairs, but it must be possible at least to talk about everything. A calculated silence about explicitly theological topics, and even more silence about structural questions, produces a mental framework of concealment and hypocritical structures. The problem is not so much one of silence as of concealment and not acknowledging what ought to be acknowledged. This is very fruitful ground for hypocrisy and brings incompetent individuals to the fore. In such circumstances, the essential mission becomes a mere holding operation and any actual substance is irrelevant, indeed all but trivial.[10]

Unquestioning loyalty to the institution can also mean disloyalty to the essence of the matter. For the typical underdog mentality, any comment on or expression of a critical opinion about a statement or pronouncement of the Catholic magisterium means that the institution has been fundamentally called in question[11] Yet the scandal is not that the authority of the institution has been contradicted. The real scandal is false loyalty, and a refusal to refer and relate to what is actually behind the statement, if necessary by contradicting it publicly.[12]

VI Closing comment

The Catholic Church in Croatia is a strong institution, and so it is understandable that the Church and what goes on inside it arouse the particular attention and special interest of the public. The public not only want to hear what the Church thinks about something but also wish that the Church would, and increasingly require the Church to, tell its own story and say what is really going on inside it, with the absolute openness demanded by the situation. But discussions of topics that concern the Church's domestic questions but have not been effectively worked through are still more or less reserved to the hierarchical part of the Church. The constantly repeated asseveration (with regard to responsibility) that the Church as such concerns all its members seems at the very least hypocritical. Croatian society remains a deeply divided community and the Catholic Church assuredly and logically also plays a part in this division, not least of all because of its practice of silence and concealment. You can't simply ask other people to change when people are perfectly entitled to require the office-holders in the Church to revise at least the way in which communication goes on inside and outside, *ad intra* and *ad extra*. As a theologian from Split said at the beginning of the present millennium: 'If you read the signs of the times attentively and want to answer the questions they raise, you soon realize that the Church itself has to change its lifestyle, which is inappropriate in so many ways. The ways in which communications, relations and procedures are managed and practised within the church community and towards those outside it have to be adapted to the new conditions of contemporary life, though without harming the fundamental structure of that community. Without this far from simple adaptation of its modes of procedure, its behaviour and its methods of communication, the Church will no longer be able to act as an effective sign of God to the world, or to operate as a saving instrument for the people of our own times'.[13]

Translated by J. G. Cumming

Notes

1. Of course this does not mean that there have been no conflicts at all. On the contrary. One of the most significant was that between the church hierarchy and the theological association known as 'Christian Presence' (Teološko društvo 'Kršćanska sadašnjost'). This was a period of very enthusiastic theological debate, especially just after the Second Vatican Council.
2. On the ambivalence of the role of the Catholic Church among the people of Croatia, see: Frano Prcela, '*Polog katoličkoga u hrvatskom identitetu*', in Zorislav Lukić & Božo Skoko (eds), *Hrvatski identitet*, Zagreb, 2011, pp. 211–32. See also the summary English version: Frano Prcela, 'Croatia: The search for identity between the conflicting priorities of nation and religion', in *Dominican Perspectives for Europe. Religion and Public Sphere*, vol. 7, Pistoia, 2011, pp. 28–34.
3. Recently, for instance, Bishop Mile Bogović gave a lecture significantly entitled 'Should the Church speak more loudly and clearly nowadays?' See: http://www.ika.hr/index.php?prikaz=vijest&ID=136705 (as at: 17 November 2011).
4. There have never been so many lay theologians in the history of the Church in this area as there are today. Nevertheless, this does not result in an improvement in dialogue within the Church or in an increased use of theology in discussions in society or interdisciplinary discourse.
5. Although a representative survey (now already more than ten years old) showed that more than two-thirds of Catholics rejected it. See: Pero Aračić, Krunoslav Nikodem & Franjo Šanjek, 'Kroatien – Eine religiöse Kultur', in:Libor Prudký & Pero Aračić (eds), *Religion und Kirchen in Ost(Mittel)Europa: Tschechien, Kroatien, Polen*, Vienna, 2001, pp. 212–19.
6. See: Frano Prcela, 'Teološki govor u postteološkom vremenu', in Frano Prcela OP & Dolores Matić OP (eds), *Sto godina nije samo prošlost. Zbornik proslave 100. obljetnice Kongregacije sestara dominikanki svetih Anđela čuvara*, Zagreb, 2007, pp. 131–43.
7. See, e. g.: Jakov Jukić, 'Hrvatski katolici u vremenu postkomunizma', in *Crkva u svijetu*, 29 (1994) 4, pp. 363–78; also Špiro Marasović, 'Perspektive pluralističkog djelovanja Crkve u hrvatskom društvu', in *Bogoslovska smotra*, 73 (2003), pp. 1–2, 361–93.
8. Instances that serve for communication with the public (episcopal press offices and press officers for church organizations) still seem to be self-serving. Of course the representatives of the Catholic hierarchy like to appear in secular media, especially if the television cameras are on them, if they think it is 'appropriate', but categorically reject any possibility of communication if the topics are 'inappropriate' or just ignore the occasions.
9. Admittedly some individuals occasionally offer a critical opinion, but their contributions are marginalized and ignored by public opinion in the Church. Consequently, to a certain extent, most of them exist as church dissidents, while a smaller number express their critical viewpoints in the course of their careers in the media, and more recently in politics, like the retired priest Ivan Grubišić, who has announced that he is standing for Parliament in Croatia.
10. Cf. Jadranka Brnčić, *Biti katolik još. Ogledi i eseji*, Zagreb, 2007, especially the chapter entitled 'Zavjera prešućivanja', pp. 149–62.
11. A good example of a non-(self-)critical relation to his themes is shown by the reaction of a representative of the church hierarchy who was asked to comment on a recently-

Silence and Concealment in the Church in Croatia

published papal document (*Dominus Iesus*), and replied that the Catholic Church in Croatia gratefully accepted everything that came from the Holy See and would not comment on it in any way. *Ibid.*, p. 218.
12. Cf. Klaus Mertes, 'Widerspruch aus Loyalität', vol. 39, Würzburg, 2009.
13. Nediljko A. Ančić, 'Prisutnost Crkve u društvu', in *Crkva u svijetu*, 36 (2001) 2, p. 125.

'Many sources are still inaccessible'

A *Concilium* interview with Hubert Wolf about Pius XII

The process for the beatification of Pius XII, already opened by Pope Paul VI in 1965, has now entered a decisive phase. On 19 December 2009, in accordance with the vote of the Congregation for the Causes of Saints (that is, the Congregation responsible for the processes of beatification and canonization), Pope Benedict XVI recognized his predecessor's 'heroic virtues'. All that is now needed for Pius XII's beatification is a miraculous cure.

Many people are still very uneasy about this particular beatification process. Both Christian and Jewish advocates as well as critics of beatifying Pius XII constantly comment on the procedure. For the most part the debate is centred on Pius XII's attitude to the Jews and his behaviour during the Holocaust.

In September 1999, John Paul II responded to Jewish historians' desire for a joint investigation of Pius XII's attitude to the National Socialist persecution of the Jews by setting up a Commission of Jewish and Catholic Historians. It was intended to examine the validity of the Vatican edition of documents of the Holy See during the Second World War (see the bibliography appended to this article) and to help to clarify certain unresolved questions. Nevertheless, two years later, in the summer of 2001, the groups of experts stopped their work because they believed that they could not carry out their task appropriately without access to the documents of the years 1939–45 in the Vatican archives. It will be possible to obtain access to the documents for this period, after cataloguing and conservation, in 2014 at the earliest.

Given this situation, is it possible to discuss the image of Eugenio Pacelli or of Pius XII in any meaningful way? Norbert Reck talked about this problem for Concilium *with the church historian Hubert Wolf, holder of the Leibniz Prize awarded by the German Research Foundation.*

CONCILIUM: *The process leading to the beatification of Pius XII is well* advanced, but is not yet concluded. You have researched Pacelli or Pius XII and published work on him, and you are Director of the Critical Online Edition of the Nuncial Reports of Eugenio Pacelli (1917–1929). What do you think we are entitled to say about him?

Hubert Wolf: It is not the historian's task to decide whether a man is Blessed, possesses heroic virtues to the requisite extent, and so on. Historians have another task in processes leading to a beatification. A commission of historians is involved in all beatification processes and canonization processes. It must assemble all accessible biographical information, traces and sources, and later swear that the *propositio* (proposal) has been fully and soundly completed. Only then does the commission of theologians pass judgement.

It is important to understand clearly the following factual point with regard to the consultation and assessment of the sources for the case of Pius XII. First of all, after the failure of the International Commission of Jewish and Catholic Historians, John Paul II decided to allow access to the archives from the pontificate of Pacelli's predecessor, Pius XI, in other words, the documents from 1922 to 1939. This occurred in two stages: 2003 and 2006. This meant that access was also granted to the documents of Eugenio Pacelli, who held the office of Nuncio in Germany and from 1929 that of Cardinal Secretary of State during this period. For that reason alone we can already consult a considerable number of new sources Finally, Benedict XVI commissioned the Vatican Archive to allow access to the archives of the pontificate of Pius XII. Another 200,000 fascicles should be available in two to three years.

As an historian I had expected that, following on the decision of Blessed John Paul II, there would be an initial delay until all sources were accessible; that these sources would be examined with composure and equanimity (*sine ira et studio*), in accordance with all historical rules; and that only then the Congregation would decide whether the requiste degree of virtue had been attained.

Does that mean that the second step has been taken before the first in this beatification process?

Here I refer only to the historian's logic. Other forms of logic and other contexts of substantiation might be invoked. But as an historian with a

Interview

certain degree of experience in commissions of historians concerned with beatifications, I know the precise counter-questions that are put to historians, and how meticulously the material has to be studied in the first place. Admittedly, I cannot be sure whether the members of the Roman Congregation for beatification and canonization processes have actually already examined the 200,000 boxes of documents, the 200,000 archival units from the pontificate of Pius XII (a considerable number of which are still not classified, as the Prefect in charge of the archives says). After all, not even the 100,000 boxes from the pontificate of Pius XI, which have now been accessible for nine years, have been really disclosed, let alone then studied thoroughly. To date I myself have seen perhaps 1000 of the toal number of boxes. In short, we are dealing with a vast body of sources in this matter.

Does this mean that it is actually far too early to say anything at all about Pius XII?

Currently the debate is intensively focussed on the Second World War, on Pius XII's supposed, factual or non-factual silence about the Holocaust. As yet not all the sources are accessible that would allow this question to be resolved definitively. But popes do not fall ready-formed from heaven. They too have biographies that begin long before they are elected pope. Therefore I would say that we have to discuss Eugenio Pacelli first of all.

In our Münster project, we are publishing an online edition (www.pacelli-edition.de) of Pacelli's close on 7000 nuncial reports from Germany between 1917 and 1929. The Leibniz Prize awarded by the German Research Foundation (Deutsche Forschungsgemeinschaft = DFG) enabled me to prepare this project carefully. It subsequently received support as a long-term project from the DFG. Pacelli sent detailed written reports to Rome, sometimes even several in the course of a day. We have not only the finished reports but the drafts. This makes it possible to compare Pacelli's spontaneous notes with the final edited texts. On each day you can follow what he thought was important, what he reported to Rome, how he saw things, his criteria, and his real impressions of Germany.

Do any patterns merge from all this?

It seems to me that Pacelli received two decisive impressions from his time in Germany. One was the trauma caused by the Kulturkampf period, that is, from the disputes between Imperial Germany and the Catholic Church from 1871 to 1878. The after-effects marked German Catholicism for many years on. But Pacelli was concerned not so much with the political contention, the anti-ecclesiastical legislation and so on, as with the associated disastrous influence on pastoral care. As a result of the conflict with the German State, thousands of parishes were without priests and bishops were expelled. Many thousands of Catholics died without the consolation of the last sacraments and the Church's most important task could not be fulfilled. Pacelli thought that ultimately God would require the Church to account for the loss of so many souls entrusted to its care. The consequence for him was that the Church should never again allow itself to be drawn into another conflict with the State. This was a German experience that proved very revealing with regard to what happened in the Second World War.

The second trauma was that of Pope Benedict XV's peace initiative of 1917. Pacelli was to negotiate with the German Government and to try to influence the process of bringing the First World War to an end. These efforts fell flat, and Pacelli came to the conclusion that in future the Holy See had to observe strict neutrality. Since there were believers on both sides in every instance, it was impossible to prefer one to the other.

These two traumas profoundly affected Pacelli during his twelve years in Germany. This probably makes it easier for us to understand why he was so very reticent later on about making public protests directed against the Nazis. He was simply different to his predecessor Pius XI, who often reacted very spontaneously. Of course, it is true to say in any discussion now of Pius XII's supposed silence about the Holocaust that in his Christmas address of 24 December 1942 he did not expressly name the murderers and their victims, but referred only to those who 'without any guilt, to some extent solely on account of their nationality or race', were subjected to a 'direct or slow death'. He expressly praised Bishop Konrad von Preysing of Berlin for his defence of the persecuted Jews, and in several letters left it to the German bishops to decide themselves what kind of episcopal intervention would be appropriate. It would be good if they did speak out. He too wanted to protest but could not do so because his papal office imposed reticence on him in this respect. We know these letters to the German bishops, which show that Pius XII himself felt that he wished to speak out, that he ought to speak out, that he should protest emphatically, but that his understanding of his office prevented him from doing so. In my opinion these statements show that these two traumas had possibly affected him lastingly.

Has evaluating Pacelli's nuncial reports changed your opinion of him?

My own initial opinion was that Pacelli as a nuncio was more of a politician, a shrewd diplomat. But my image of him has become more nuanced. The sources disclose this firm insistence on pastoral care as the supreme commandment (*cura animarum suprema lex*). It may not always be a judicious choice to keep to this principle in the political sphere. But of course as a pastor he had no other choice. But this is no more than a preliminary impression, for we still haven't edited, let alone analyzed, all 7000 nuncial reports.

What role did Pacelli play in the negotiations for the Concordat between the Holy See and the German Reich?

As is well-known, Pacelli has been accused of making a deal with Hitler. In order to ensure Hitler's approval of the Concordat, Pacelli is said to have offered him an assurance that the Catholic Centre Party (*Zentrumspartei*) would agree in Parliament to the Enabling Act (*Ermächtigungsgesetz*) which cancelled the Weimar Constitution and gave Hitler extraordinary powers. In that case Pacelli would have helped Hitler to achieve a majority in the apparent legitimation of his dictatorship. But the sources that we have seen contradict this hypothesis unequivocally. The opposite was true. Pacelli was disturbed by the fact that on 24 March 1933 the Catholic Centre Party had agreed to the Enabling Act and four days later the German bishops withdrew the condemnation of National Socialism. By doing this the German Catholics so to speak deprived Pacelli of the only two trump cards he had in his negotiations with Hitler about the Concordat.

There are several other examples that can be taken as showing that Pacelli often failed to accord with the generalized clichés used to characterize him. With these questions we are always focussing on Germany. But the Catholic Church is a global player. We have to ask international questions and to concern ourselves (a far too rare event) with the pontificate of Pius XI and that of Pius XII in an international context. If we can't place him in this international complex our understanding of the relevant issues thereafter will be only partial. An American or Canadian, a

Latin American or East European researcher, pursuing his questions through the sources, will emphasize quite different aspects of the problem.

How would you describe your interests with regard to Pius XII?

I have neither apologetical nor polemical intentions in my concern with Pacelli or Pius XII. I have only questions, open questions. For instance: how exactly does the Curia arrive at its decisions? This question has never been posed appropriately to date. Does the Pope alone really make the decisions? In that case he alone would bear the responsibility for them. Even under Pius XI the directive style of the papacy became increasingly autocratic. In fact, the 'Sacred Congregation for Extraordinary Ecclesiastical Affairs', subordinate to the Secretariat of State and consisting of seven cardinals, was no longer convoked under Pius XI. Moreover, from 1944 to 1952 Pius XII did not appoint a Secretary of State. Accordingly I ask who exactly works to the Pope. Who prepares the decisions? This is a profoundly interesting but hitherto open question, because of course decisions must be differently classified depending on how the decision-making process is conducted.

Does that mean that in general we are far too inclined to project a number of things onto the man at the top?

Indeed. If you examine actual decision processes more precisely, you are faced with quite different questions. For instance, why did the encyclical *Societatis unio* on the 'unity of the human race' never appear? Pius XI commissioned it and and it contains – at least in Father Gustav Gundlach's German draft, a clear condemnation of anti-Semitism. Of course we have to ask why it did not appear? Did Pacelli as Cardinal Secretary of State just not present the sick pope with the finished encylical? Was the matter simply filed away when Pacelli himself was elected pope? Because he did not agree with it? That is constantly suggested. But we have no proof whatsoever of this. Should I make a judgment now before really inspecting all relevant sources? It would be a harsh verdict indeed to opine that the Secretary of State held back from his Pope an encyclical which that very pope had commissioned. You have to be in possession of incontrovertible facts in order to maintain this. And we don't have those facts. But we continue to address the question.

Interview

Nevertheless the question whether Pacelli or Pius was anti-Jewish is particularly important if the Church beatifies him and thereby singles him out as a model for all Christians...

Yet again we have to say that the question can be answered only when we have access to all the sources. There are actually scarcely any statements against the Jews that might properly be characterized as anti-Semitic in the nuncial reports up to 1929. But for the moment we can say what kind of pattern influenced Pacelli in that he was not wholly unaffected by traditional anti-Jewish Catholicism. We are all aware of the Good Friday prayer in the Latin rite of the time: 'Let us pray also for the unbelieving Jews: that our God and Lord will remove the veil from their hearts, so that they too may acknowledge our Lord Jesus Christ.' ('Oremus et pro perfidis Judaeis: ut Deus et Dominus noster auferat velamen de cordibus eorum; ut et ipsi agnoscant Jesus Christum Dominum nostrum'). In 1928, when the priests' association *Amici Israel* ('Friends of Israel') proposed that this prayer should be revised, Pacelli did not take up the idea. He reported the suggestion accurately but did not espouse it.

So it is true to say that Pacelli did not commit himself in this respect, and remained in the same old rut of traditional anti-Judaism. But surely this incident says more about Catholic anti-Jewish attitudes than about Pacelli?

To be sure, we don't know why Pacelli was reluctant to commit himself in this regard. So far we have come across no statements on the subject. But the revision of the Good Friday prayer for the Jews would have been a real change of line. Just think. This was an area for which the Church was solely responsible, for it concerned its liturgy, the way in which it represented itself in Catholic services all over the world. No state affairs of any kind were in question and no partner in any Concordat was needed to change the formula. In this case, it was the responsibility of the Church pure and simple to get rid of the anti-Jewish prayer. Instead, the *Amici Israel* were prohibited under Pius XI.

I am constantly surprised that the significance of this initiative is so underestimated. We mustn't forget that 5000 priests, bishops and even cardinals supported the *Amici Israel* in 1928 and wanted to revise this liturgical prayer with its anti-Semitic undertones. Finally, even the Sacred

Congregation of Rites voted unanimously to change the liturgy at this point. This proves that there were also respectful and not only anti-Jewish attitudes in the Catholic Church and in the Curia. The arguments put forward by *Amici Israel* were indeed conclusive, as one of the assessors, Abbot Ildefons Schuster, and later Archbishop of Milan, explained: the word 'perfidus', which originally signified a lack in theology, had become a source of misunderstanding in modern usage, for when they heard it most people would interpret *perfidis Iudaeis* merely as 'perfidious Jews'. This had to be taken into account and the term 'perfidus' had to be removed from the prayer.

Marco Sales and Rafael Merry del Val of the Holy Office decisively opposed this proposal, to some extent with paranoid anti-Zionist accusations. If today the Zionists were to found the State of Israel, then tomorrow they will cross the sea in their ships and destroy Rome. It seems scarcely credible that they could have entertained such delusions. Finally Merry del Val and Pius XI formulated a decree that was published on 14 March 1928. It prohibited the *Amici Israel* group and condemned racial anti-Semitism as unchristian. A white smoke bomb indeed, for the Pope's thinking was: if it ever gets out that we prevented the revision of the Good Friday petition, it might be interpreted as anti-Semitism. Therefore it would be better to condemn anti-Semitism at the same time. The bishops and faithful were quite unaware of this background. The decree said nothing about the Good Friday prayer for the Jews. All it said was that the *Amici Israel* had offended against the teaching of the Church and the sacred liturgy in some way. Yet nowadays this decree is constantly cited to show that the Catholic Church had condemned racial anti-Semitism much earlier than all the others.

I find this sequence of events quite decisive. In this case the charge is to be laid against Pius XI, and not the much-maligned Pius XII. Pius XI must have had reasons for persisting in opposing the initiative for revision irrespective of the fact that it had so many supporters. This takes me back to the point that if you want to pronounce on the silence of the Church about the Holocaust, then you also have to say something about the behaviour of the Curia and the attitude of the Church to the Jews in a much wider context. Then I see 1928 as the squandering of a real opportunity. If the revision had been made in 1928, the Church would have been in a much more preferable position well in advance of future conflicts. But a church historian can't deal with 'had beens' and 'would have beens'.

So there is much more at issue than finding who was guilty of specific things.

That is true, and it is true of Pius XI as well. His position in 1938 was quite different to that of 1933 or 1928. In the last text, which he wrote himself, to the cardinals of the USA and Canada, he spoke on behalf of the Jewish students in all faculties who had been excluded from universities in Germany, Austria and Italy for racial reasons. Accordingly, he asked the cardinals to find corresponding places for these students to continue their studies in the USA and Canada, because they had the same honourable 'razza' as our Saviour Jesus Christ.

In this respect, too, we can ask what Pacelli's position was. We know very little about this, but it is important. Of course I undertand that we would all like to answer the final question now: Did he say nothing or did he not keep silence? Did he think of talking out? But we have to start by looking much farther back. When did he know something? Who told him? How trustworthy was his information? Who did he discuss the subject with? Are there documents of Vatican provenance corresponding to the written material which we know of from the ambassadors?

I do not claim to say that talking out would have been more just. That too would be a moral question. I am more interested in the actual historical circumstances, the actual state of information. And so the first thing I would do would be to furnish a crystal-clear chronology showing what was known of whom when. Then we could at least say, on the basis of the nuncial reports, what the state of his information was on this day or that or five days later ... But I can only do that when I have evaluated all the sources.

And even then we have still said nothing about Pacelli's theology; nothing therefore about the encyclical *Mystici Corporis*, or his approval of historico-critical exegesis, or the 1950 dogma of Mary's bodily assumption into heaven, which is an immense topic in its own right.

So there is still much research to be done...

The decisive pronouncements about Pius XII in current circulation still fall very short of being anything more than hypotheses. There are still a vast number of open questions and an immense number of unexplored sources. There is much to be done. I devoutly wish that an international research effort could be made with regard to Pius as the global player he certainly was in order to make sure that the result is truly comprehensive. We are a long way from achieving that in the world of historians.

Translated by J. G. Cumming

Select bibliography

Pierre Blet, Angelo Martini, Burkhard Schneider & Robert Graham (eds), *Actes et Documents du Saint-Siège relatifs à la Seconde Guerre Mondiale* [The Acts and Documents of the Holy See Relative to World War II], 11 vols, Vatican City, 1965–81.

Burkhard Schneider (ed.), *Die Briefe Pius' XII. an die deutschen Bischöfe*, Mainz, 1966.

Hubert Wolf, *Papst und Teufel. Die Archive des Vatikan und das Dritte Reich*, Munich, 2008.

Hubert Wolf & Klaus Unterburger, 'Papst Pius XII. und die Juden. Zum Stand der Forschung', in: *Theologische Revue* 105 (2009/4), pp. 265–80.

A Tribute to Paul Burns

Paul Burns, latterly the indefatigable editor of the English edition of *Concilium* during its publication by SCM Press, and known to many of its publishers, editors and contributors across the world as a responsible colleague and delightful friend with a profound interest in community and the future of a just and liberal Church, died suddenly in January 2012.

Paul was educated by the Benedictines at Ampleforth and read modern languages at Oxford, where he specialized in Spanish with French as a subsidiary subject. He was a writer, editor, accomplished painter in watercolour and gouache, creative gardener, choir member, literary and scholarly translator, ecumenist, school governor, and of course a devoted father of four children, but essentially a publisher. He was consistent in seeing religious publishing as an intellectually, socially and morally responsible vocation that also called for fun, joy and celebration. This combination sometimes aroused the ire of bores and fundamentalists, ecclesiastical and secular. Although he spent a few years here and there with secular publishers, notably Paul Hamlyn and Peter Sackett, and made children's book publishing one of his other interests, Paul's career was essentially bound up with modern Catholic publishing, and above all with Burns & Oates, Britain's premier Catholic publishing house, in several of its manifestations. Paul's career effectively started when he became production manager under his uncle Tom Burns at the old Burns & Oates in Ashley Place, Westminster, and nurtured a respect for the great typographical traditions of the firm from Meynell to Morrison that he never lost. He was managing director during the short-lived rule of the German firm Herder of Freiburg and supervised a number of landmark successes of the Vatican II period in the 1960s, such as the *New Catechism* (the epoch-making and crudely censored 'Dutch Catechism'), the six-volume theological encylopaedia *Sacramentum Mundi* edited by Karl Rahner and company, and forward-looking journals such as the English edition of the international *Concilium*, which shared the influences of Karl Rahner, Hans Küng and Edward Schillebeeckx, the English *Herder Correspondence* and the new critical monthly *Catholic Education Today*. Shortly before Herder's withdrawal from British publishing, and enthralled by the reforms and prospects of Vatican II, Paul also planned an exciting but over-ambitious English liturgical project with scant attention to church authorities, and with typical enthusiasm even engaged choirs to record new church music and brilliant new liturgical texts. This anticipation of the mind of the Church proved intolerable to Westminster and was abruptly halted.

Paul was not a political publisher through association with a particular party, but a convinced anti-fascist who deprecated his family's direct support for the rebel rather than the loyalist side in the Spanish Civil War. He was shocked to discover only a few years ago that his Jesuit uncle had volunteered to join Franco as a chaplain for the rebels. His strong sense of justice and fairness made him an advocate of liberation theology and the option for the poor in Latin America and through committed action where possible in the world. He translated from Spanish, Portuguese, French and Italian, and edited and published a vast number of works of liberation theology, including an important series of classics in this area, many of which he translated himself, as well as countless articles for *Concilium* over the years. A notable achievement which raised sacred eyebrows was his translation of Hugo Assmann's *Practical Theology of Liberation*, which appeared with reproductions of Masereel's classic woodcut illustrations for the *Communist Manifesto* of Marx and Engels.

His vision was international and ecumenical within and outside Catholic publishing. He inspired and coordinated the ecumenical symposia for religious publishers held at Spode House, the former Dominican conference centre, and organized many fruitful meetings and dinners of religious publishers at the Frankfurt Book Fair and elsewhere. Wherever he lived, he played a major part in ecumenical groups which he often founded. For a time, Paul with a friend directed his own production house, which conceived and packaged forward-looking religious books for leading British, Irish and US publishers, including the important symposia *The Church Now* and *The Bible Now*, which he co-edited, a series of new translations of spiritual classics, and an anthology of totally new prayers commissioned from authors such as Graham Greene, George Barker and John Heath-Stubbs.

Later, Paul returned to Burns & Oates when Search Press finally acquired the imprint from Herder, and assumed a new role as editorial director. It was then that he devised, edited and produced what was probably his most important project, the twelve-volume revision of *Butler's Lives of the Saints* by himself and a company of reforming authors. This was a courageous attempt to follow and even improve on the Church's own moderately severe culling of fictitious saints from its liturgical books, and to tell something of the truth about the survivors and the immense number of new saints created especially by Pope John Paul II. For a time Paul continued to work as adviser to Burns & Oates when the imprint was acquired by the new conglomerate Continuum, and was eventually asked to edit the English-language *Concilium* by its present publishers SCM Press. Just before he died, Paul was working on the first 2012 issue, communicating with the editors in various countries, with the publishers, and with the new coordinating office in Madras, India.

Paul's special combination of high seriousness, compassion and often uproariously good humour was always rare in religious publishing and will be sorely missed.

Contributors

REGINA AMMICHT QUINN studied Catholic theology and German literature. She is a Professor at the International Centre for Ethics in Science (IZEW) at the University of Tübingen. Her publications include *Von Lissabon bis Auschwitz: Zum Paradigmawechsel in der Theodizeefrage* (Freiburg im Breisgau, 1992); *Körper, Religion und Sexualität: Theologische Reflexion zur Ethik der Geschlechter*, (Mainz, ^{3}2004); *Glück – der Ernst des Lebens* (Freiburg im Breisgau, 2006); 'Living with Losses: The Crisis in the "Christian West"', in: James F. Keenan (ed.), *Catholic theological Ethics: Past, Present, and Future. The Trento Conference* (New York, 2011), pp. 60–9.

Address: Prof. Dr. Regina Ammicht Quinn, Eberhard Karls University, Tübingen, International Centre for Ethics in the Sciences and Humanities (IZEW), Section Ethics and Culture (director), Wilhelmstraße 19, 72074 Tübingen, Germany.
Tel.: +49 (0) 7071 / 29 77988 or 29 77517.
Fax: +49 (0) 7071 / 29 5255
Email: regina.ammicht-quinn@uni-tuebingen.de

AGENOR BRIGHENTI Agenor Brighenti is Brazilian. He has a doctorate in Theological and Religious Sciences from the Catholic University of Louvain, Belgium. He is currently Research Professor at the Pontifical Catholic University of Curitiba, Brazil, President of the National Pastoral Institute of the Brazilian Bishops' Conference, visiting professor at the Pontifical University of Mexico and at the Latin American Episcopal Council's Institute of Pastoral Theology. He is the author of over 100 articles and dozens of books, including: *A pastoral dá o que pensar. A inteligência da prática transformadora da fé*, Ed. Paulinas, Brazil (2006) & Ed. Dabar, Mexico; *Para compreender o Documento de Aparecida. O pré-texto, o con-texto e o texto*, Paulinas, Brazil (2007) & Dabar, Mexico; *A Igreja Perplexa. A novas perguntas, novas respostas,* Paulinas, Brazil (2004), &Ed. Palabram, Mexico.

Contributors

Address: Agenor Brighenti, Rua João Dranka, 66 Apto. 1002, Bairro Cristo Rei,80050-530 CURITIBA, Paraná, Brazil
Email: agenor.brighenti@pucpr.br

JAMES A. CORIDEN is a priest of the Diocese of Gary. He received a doctorate in Canon Law from the Gregorian University in Rome and a doctorate in Civil Law from the Catholic University of America in Washington. He is Professor of Church Law and Dean Emeritus at the Washington Theological Union. He has written many articles on canonical issues. His most recent book is *The Rights of Catholics in the Church* (New York, 2007).

Address: Washington Theological Union, 6896 Laurel Street, N.W., Washington, DC, 20012, USA.
Telephone: 202-541-5243, Fax: 202-726-1716
Email: coriden@wtu.edu

GEORG EVERS was born in 1936. He studied under Karl Rahner and was awarded a doctorate in the theology of religion. He was in charge of the Asia desk in the Institute of Missiology, Aachen, Germany from 1979 to 2001. He made several visits to Asian countries under the auspices of the Institute and took part in important theological conferences in the context of the Union of Asian Bishops' Conferences (FABC). He has published numerous works on interreligious dialogue and mission theology.

SOLANGE LEFEBVRE is Professor of Theology and Religious Studies at the University of Montreal, Canada, and Chair,. She teaches religion, culture and society. She has published works on ages and generations (Fides, Paulist, 1992–5), including *Cultures et spiritualités des jeunes* (Bellarmin, 2008), and numerous books and articles on secularism and religion in the public sphere: *La religion dans la sphère publique* (Presses de l'Université de Montréal, 2005); *Le Patrimoine religieux du Québec* (Presses de l'Université Laval, 2009).

Address: Faculté de théologie et de science des religions, Université de Montréal, C. P. 6128 Succursale centre-ville, Montréal, Québec, Canada H3C 3J7.
Email: solange.lefebvre@umontreal.ca

ELOI MESSI METOGO OP was born in Cameroun in 1952 .He holds a degree in literature, doctorates in theology and another doctrate in history of religions and religious anthropology. He teaches Christology and theological anthropology at the Catholic University of Central Africa in Yaoundé. His publications include *Éléments pour une théologie africaine pour le XXIe siècle* (Yaoundé, 2005), and his most recent work is : 'L'enjeu de Dieu en Afrique', in Ambroise Kom (ed.), *Fabien Eboussi Boulaga, l'audace de penser* (Paris, 2010).

Address: Professor Eloi Messi Metogo OP, Université catholique d'Afrique Centrale, BP 11628, Yaoundé, Cameroun
Fax : (237) 230 55 01, fax: (237) 22 30 55 01, Tel: (237) 99 12 47 06
Email: eloimessi@yahoo.fr

PETER C. PHAN emigrated from Vietnam to the United States in 1975. He currently holds the Ignacio Ellacuria Chair of Catholic Social Thought at Georgetown University. He has been awarded three doctorates by thesis and two honorary doctorates. He has written or edited some 30 books and 300 essays. He specializes in systematic theology, missiology, interculturation and interreligious dialogue. In 2010, he was awarded the John Courtney Murray Award by the Catholic Theological Society of America for outstanding achievements in theology.

Email: pcp5@georgetown.edu

FRANO PRCELA OP was born in Sinj, Croatia, in 1966. He is a scientific research assistant at the Institut M.-Dominique Chenu in Berlin. His publications include 'Die "Kirche der kroatischen Märtyrer". Von Opfern zu Märtyrern und zurück', *Wort und Antwort* 52 (2011) 3, pp. 125–30; 'Croatia: The search for identity between the conflicting priorities of nation

and religion', *Dominican Perspectives for Europe–Religion and Public Sphere*, vol. 7, Pistoia, 2011, pp. 28–34.
Email: franoprcela@yahoo.com

NORBERT RECK was born in 1961. He edits the German edition of *Concilium*. The main focus of his theological work is the treatment of victims and perpetrators of crimes in former dictatorships. His publications include: *Abenteuer Gott: Den christlichen Glauben neu denken* (2003), *Hanna Mandel: Beim Gehen entsteht der Weg* (2008).

Address: Arndtstrasse 5, 80469 Munich, Germany
Email: norbert.reck@mnet-mail.de.

SUSAN A. ROSS is Professor and Chair of the theology department at Loyola University, Chicago. She is the author of *Extravagant Affections: A Feminist Sacramental Theology* (1998), *For the Beauty of the Earth: Women, Sacramentality, and Justice* (2006), and the forthcoming *Anthropology: Seeking Light and Beauty*. She is President-Elect of the Catholic Theological Society of America.

Address: Prof. Susan Ross, Loyola University of Chicago, 6525 N. Sheridan Road, Chicago, IL 60626, USA
Email: sross@luc.edu

LUIZ CARLOS SUSIN is Professor of Systematic Theology at the Pontifical Catholic University of Rio Grande do Sul and at the Higher School of Theology and Franciscan Spirituality, both in Porto Alegre, Brazil. He is an ex-President of the Brazilian Society for Theology and Religious Studies, and Secretary General of the World Forum for Theology and Liberation. His recent research has been into the relationship between theology and ecology. His publications include *A Criação de Deus* (2003); *Deus, Pai, Filho e Espirito Santo; Jesus, Filho de Deus e Filho de Maria; Assim na terre como no céu,* some published by Paulinas (São Paulo) and some by Vozes (Petrópolis).

Contributors

Address: Prof. Dr. L.C. Susin, Rua Juarez Távora, 171, 91520-100 - Porto Alegre (RS), Brazil.

Email: lcsusin@pucrs.br

ANDRÉS TORRES QUEIRUGA was born in 1940 and was till his retirement in 2011 professor of philosophy of religion at the University of Santiago de Compostela. He describes his main concerns as (1) applying the idea of 'the God who creates out of love' to the main theological topics and (2) commitment to an 'evangelically democratic' renewal of church order. His many published works include *Constitución y evolución del dogma* (1977); *Recuperar la salvación* (1977, ^{3}2001); *Creo en Dios Padre* (^{5}1998); *Recuperar la creación* (1997; German trans. 2008); *Fin del cristianismo premoderno* (2000); *Repensar la resurrección* (2003); *Esperanza a pesar del mal* (2005); *Repensar la revelación* (2008; revised ed. of 1977, trans. into Italian, Portuguese and German); *Repensar el mal: De la ponerología a la teodicea* (2011).

Address: Facultade de Filosofia. 15782 Santiago de Compostela. Spain (Private: O Curraliño, 23-G. 15705 Santiago de Compostela. Spain) E-mail: torresqueiruga@gmail.com

FELIX WILFRED is founder–director of the Asian Centre for Cross-Cultural Studies. He is a member of the Statutory Ethical Committee of the Indian Institute of Technology (IIT), Chennai. Earlier he was Professor and President of the Faculty of Arts and Chairman of the School of Philosophy and Religious Thought at the University of Madras. He was also Professor and head of the department of Christian Studies in the same university. Dr Wilfred is the President of the International Theological Review *Concilium*. He has been a member of the Vatican International Theological Commission and visiting professor in several universities, including the University of Frankfurt, University of Nijmegen, Boston College, Ateneo de Manila and Fudan University, China. His writings have appeared in French, German, Italian, Spanish, Portuguese and Chinese. In 2008, a Festschrift was published in his honour with 47 contributions by scholars from 20 countries. The Government of India has appointed him to

Contributors

the Chair of Indic Religion and South Asian Diaspora at Trinity College, Dublin, Ireland.

E-mail: felixwilfred@gmail.com

HUBERT WOLF was born in 1959. He is Professor of Medieval and Modern Church History at the University of Münster. He studied Catholic theology at the Universities of Tübingen and Munich. He was ordained in 1985 and worked as a parish priest in the diocese of Rottenburg–Stuttgart until 1990. In 2003 he was awarded the Leibniz Prize, Germany's most highly-remunerated research award, for his outstanding scholarly achievement. In 2004, he received the Communicator Prize for the exemplary way in which he conveyed scholarship to the public. He was given the Gutenberg Prize in 2006. His publications include: *Inquisition, Index, Zensur: Wissenskulturen der Neuzeit im Widerstreit* (Paderborn, 2001); *Index: Der Vatikan und die verbotenen Bücher* (Munich, 2006); *Die Affäre Sproll – Die Rottenburger Bischofswahl 1926/27 und ihre Hintergründe* (Ostfildern, 2009).

Address: Seminar für Mittlere und Neuere Kirchengeschichte, Johannisstraße 8–10, 48143 Münster, Germany.
Email: hubert.wolf@uni-muenster.de.

CONCILIUM
International Journal of Theology

FOUNDERS
Anton van den Boogaard; Paul Brand; Yves Congar, OP; Hans Küng; Johann Baptist Metz; Karl Rahner, SJ; Edward Schillebeeckx

BOARD OF DIRECTORS
President: Felix Wilfred
Vice Presidents: Erik Borgman; Diego Irarrázaval; Susan Ross

BOARD OF EDITORS
Regina Ammicht Quinn (Frankfurt, Germany)
Maria Clara Bingemer (Rio de Janeiro, Brazil)
Erik Borgman (Nijmegen, The Netherlands)
Lisa Sowle Cahill (Boston, USA)
Dennis Gira (Paris, France)
Hille Haker (Frankfurt, Germany)
Diego Irarrázaval (Santiago, Chile)
Solange Lefebvre (Montreal, Canada)
Eloi Messi Metogo (Yaounde, Cameroon)
Sarojini Nadar (Durban, South Africa)
Daniel Franklin Pilario (Quezon City, Philippines)
Susan Ross (Chicago, USA)
Silvia Scatena (Reggio Emilia, Italy)
Jon Sobrino SJ (San Salvador, El Salvador)
Luiz Carlos Susin (Porto Alegre, Brazil)
Andres Torres Queiruga (Santiago de Compostela, Spain)
Marie-Theres Wacker (Münster, Germany)
Felix Wilfred (Madras, India)

PUBLISHERS
SCM Press (London, UK)
Matthias-Grünewald Verlag (Ostfildern, Germany)
Editrice Queriniana (Brescia, Italy)
Editorial Verbo Divino (Estella, Spain)
EditoraVozes (Petropolis, Brazil)
Ex Libris and Synopsis (Rijeka, Croatia)

Concilium Secretariat:
Asian Centre for Cross-Cultural Studies,
40/6A, Panayur Kuppam Road, Sholinganallur Post, Panayur, Madras 600119, India.
Phone: +91- 44 24530682 Fax: +91- 44 24530443
E-mail: Concilium.madras@gmail.com
Managing Secretary: Jayashree Narasimhan

Concilium Subscription Information

February   2012/1: *Sacramentalizing Human History*

April   2012/2: *Theology and Magisterium*

August   2012/3: *Vatican II*

October   2012/4: *Gender and Theology*

December   2012/5: *Water*

New subscribers: to receive *Concilium 2012* (five issues) anywhere in the world, please copy this form, complete it in block capitals and send it with your payment to the dress below.

Please enter my subscription for *Concilium 2012*

Individuals
____ £45.00 UK
____ £85.00 overseas and Eire
____ $135.00 North America/Rest of World
____ €110.00 Europe

Institutions
____ £65.00 UK
____ £105.00 overseas and Eire
____ $175 North America/Rest of World
____ €135.00 Europe

Postage included – airmail for overseas subscribers

Payment Details:
Payment must accompany all orders and can be made by cheque or credit card
I enclose a cheque for £/$/€ _____ Payable to Hymns Ancient and Modern Ltd
Please charge my Visa/MasterCard (Delete as appropriate) for £/$/€ _____

Credit card number _____

Expiry date _____

Signature of cardholder _____

Name on card _____

Telephone _____ E-mail _____

Send your order to *Concilium,* **Hymns Ancient and Modern Ltd**
13a Hellesdon Park Road, Norwich NR6 5DR, UK
E-mail: concilium@hymnsam.co.uk
or order online at www.conciliumjournal.co.uk

Customer service information
All orders must be prepaid. Subscriptions are entered on an annual basis (i.e. January to December). No refunds on subscriptions will be made after the first issue of the Journal has been despatched. If you have any queries or require Information about other payment methods, please contact our Customer Services department.

CPSIA information can be obtained at www.ICGtesting.com
Printed in the USA
BVOW040548300812

299214BV00013B/1/P